KATIE BROWN

ENTERTAINS

KATIE BROWN

ENTERTAINS

16 MENUS 16 OCCASIONS 16 TABLES

Written with Catherine Lippman

Photography by Paul Whicheloe

Design by Dina Dell'Arciprete Houser

HarperResource

An Imprint of HarperCollins*Publishers*

HarperCollins books may be purchased for educational, business, or sales promotional use.

For information please write: Special Markets Department, HarperCollins Publishers Inc., 10 East 53rd Street,

New York, NY 10022.

FIRST EDITION

Designed by Dina Dell'Arciprete Houser

Printed on acid-free paper

Photographs © 2000 by Paul Whicheloe

Library of Congress Cataloging-in-Publication Data

Brown, Katie.

Katie Brown entertains : 16 menus, 16 occasions, 16 tables / Katie Brown.—1st ed.

p. cm.

ISBN 0-06-271615-8

1. Entertaining. 2. Cookery. 3. Menus. I. Title.

TX731 .B76 2000

642.4—dc21 00–039633

00 01 02 03 04 RRD 10 9 8 7 6 5 4 3 2 1

This book is dedicated to my grandfather

PRENTISS MARSH BROWN

Thank you for our trips to Wing-Dings in your Cadillac for pink peppermint patties.

Thank you for your Indian stories, cardigan sweaters, great fires,

Sunday night waffle dinners, and for building a bridge where there wasn't one.

Thank you for inspiring me.

contents

Acknowledgments

This book has required the time, devotion, sacrifice, faith, and love of many wonderful and talented people. It is overwhelming to me when I look back and think of all that I have been given.

LET ME BEGIN BY SAYING THANK YOU TO . . .

My Uncle Meredith Hyatt for always knowing I would.

My mother, Meg Brown, for telling me "You love to eat, you'll learn to cook."

My father, Paul Brown, for telling me "You can be a diver without a diving board."

My sister Marlee Brown for truly being my angel.

My sister Lynn Brown for her unflappable strength.

My brother Bing Brown for his originality.

My brother-in-law Bob Stefanski for dealing with agents, being wise, and negotiating me onto TV.

My brother-in-law Dan Musser for giving me the Grand Hotel Pecan Balls.

MY UNBELIEVABLE, DEDICATED, HARDWORKING, AND HILARIOUS STAFF:

Catherine Lippman: You will never know how lucky I feel that you came into my life when you did. The ways you have influenced this book and my business are unmeasurable . . . you are the person that I could never have done without this past year:

Kerri Mertaugh, for moving lock, stock, and barrel in four days and for not stopping until the last day of shooting.

Shannon Murphy, for being the best U-Haul partner ever; for always being fun, willing, and eager no matter how many days you had gone without sleep and for saying; "Whatever it takes."

Sarah Mastracco, for convincing me not to make Jell-O.

Liv Grey, for jumping right onto a fast-moving train and giving us a big dose of professionalism.

Joe Lucas, for having an incredible sense of humor and great taste.

Robert Hamm and Bette Torjanaski, for all the hours, all the laughs, and all the understanding.

AND TO:

Dina Dell'Arciprete for speaking my language and designing a book that is so right for me.

Paul Whicheloe for never saying "no" or "enough" and for taking photographs that brought our food and tables to a new level.

TO MY FRIENDS:

Sarah, for being my muse, for being my partner in GOAT, and for being my very first friend.

Jen, Marge, Nancy, Mariska, and Tori, for hanging in there with me.

My dog, Doris, for being happy to see me, even when my schedule made her suffer.

Bobby Flay, for holding my hand and helping me understand how it all works.

To Kim Witherspoon, for listening to the curry story at least ten times, and for steering me in the right direction.

To my lawyers, Patti Felker and Fred Toczek, for your guidance, understanding, and creative thinking; I feel so much safer with you on my side.

To Marion Manaker, for recognizing that I had a book, for telling me I could do anything I put my mind to, for encouraging me, staying with me, listening to me, and never doubting me.

To Meaghan Dowling, Cathy Hemming, Adrian Zackheim, and everyone at HarperCollins for providing the right environment to create a successful book.

To Marian Effinger, for caring.

To Dawn Tarnofsky and Lifetime Television, for being generous and patient while I learned how to be a person on a TV show. Thanks for giving me the opportunity to get started.

To my mother in TV, Beth Sosin, who had so much faith in me that it still takes my breath away.

To Gina Babiglia, for finding me all the way on Mackinac Island.

To Lisa Bourgouian, for teaching me how to breathe in front of the camera; "Talent's Ready."

To Van Carlson, his crew, and Saundra Jordan, for always making me look good and for truly being on my side.

To IKEA and All Clad, for providing me with the tools to use when creating this book.

To Kitchen Aid, Cynthia Parrott, and Brian Maynard, for never saying no and for giving me big and small appliances to keep my kitchens going.

To Lenox China/Lenox Brands and Peter Cobuzzi, Denise Dinyon and the Lenox Team, for allowing your china, flatware, and crystal to decorate my tables and making them sparkle. This book would not be the same without your products.

To Michelle Pierce, for being the first to show me what being a professional meant (sorry I was not ready).

TO MY HEROES:

Lee Bailey, The *Silver Palette* cookbooks, Martha Stewart, *Moosewood Cookbook,* and *Hollyhocks and Radishes,* for just being good.

Kenny Kalbacher, for making my house a home and my workshop workable, and to your family, for always taking Doris, no questions asked.

Eric Hughes, for quite simply saving the day.

Introduction

It is my favorite thing and ever since I can remember it has always been my favorite thing. Smells from the kitchen . . . friends ringing doorbells . . . family being together . . . and it all centers around the table. To celebrate . . . to break bread. Who sits where, who speaks too loudly, who falls asleep and wakes up just in time for dessert. People you love and people you are just getting to know. This is one of the things in life that is not wrong. This is one of the things that makes life good . . . really good.

My lust for entertaining began with my mother. Her ability to make the house buzz by inviting all my fellow ski racers for dinner the night before a competition. Her Christmas Eve buffets, where it seemed to me our entire town dropped by. Her "holy ladies," as my dad called them, who organized retreats and potluck suppers at our United Methodist Church on Mitchell Street. To top if off, she wouldn't let us walk to school until we had finished our home-cooked breakfast—soft boiled eggs presented in glass hens, ginger pancakes with lemon sauce, my Aunt Ruth's cinnamon bread. . . .

Food meant love and a party meant you could celebrate. My infatuation with food and entertaining continued at our family cottage on top of a hill on Marquette Island, Michigan. A cottage which my grandfather bought years ago for his family and continues to be the place where my twelve aunts and uncles and thirty-two first cousins congregate. A cottage where women cooked and swapped recipes and bragged about how many people they had for supper the night before. The men cut wood for the fireplace, played "pounce" (great card game), and kept the boat engines humming. Aunt Peggy selected just the right china to go with the yellow flowers. Aunt Nan created the kids' table (she said it provided for more peace and quiet at the big table). Aunt Barb was famous for her generous use of butter and sugar. You had to be big and strong to keep up with all the Evashevski boys and their appetites. It was not a time to be shy, but to help yourself . . . or no mashed potatoes for you.

All grown up I find myself on the shores of the Pacific, rather than the beaches of Lake Michigan . . . no family . . . no cottage . . . no ski team . . . no home-cooked food . . . what to do? That's when my next tradition began. I started a catering company, which evolved into an antique store and café—Goat. My partner and best friend Sarah and I would transform Goat into a supper club every Friday night. I would reinvent my family meals by taking thirty reservations, putting a big long table down the center of the store, and serving a four-course family style meal for all . . . *it wasn't wrong*. The hum of my guests, the second helpings. I had started my first tradition. I had created my own version of my home away from home.

I wrote this book to encourage others to start their own traditions. To help others find their own way to celebrate. I wanted to share my belief that happiness occurs over a well-planned table. The following pages are full of many projects, recipes, and "over-the-top" tabletops. I encourage mixing and matching. . . . I rarely specify measurements and I keep the size and quantities sparse, so they can be molded to suit individual desires and needs. The tables are meant to motivate and inspire . . . not to dictate. The size of the plywood, the color of paint, and the place cards should be right for you, your party, your table, your celebration. This is not an assignment book that will take away all your fun. Use these images as starting points and let your imagination soar. There are no rules or regulations. I give you my simple recipes with common ingredients and preparation that is deliberately easy. The food is basic and yummy, without having to sacrifice too much time and money. Put yourself in your creation and invite others to enjoy.

But always remember when you invite people over it is your responsibility to make them feel at home. To me, the best way to do that is to let your imperfections show. Allow your human side to emerge by holding up your mistakes proudly and inviting all to find the fun in your attempt. There is nothing more welcoming and endearing then something homemade, so why be afraid to let it look homemade. I tried to illustrate this philosophy throughout this book. In the following pages, you will see things cut unevenly, pie crusts that are imperfect as they come out of the oven, tabletops that may be a bit crooked. I wanted the styling to be minimal. I wanted the photographs real and homespun. I hope this book inspires everyone to try . . . sometimes things come out backward, but hopefully you've had fun and made some discoveries along the way. At times the tables are rough, at times not perfect, even obviously flawed. . . . I hope this will entice the reluctant entertainer to rethink entertaining at home. By embracing my imperfections, I hope to encourage others to feel at home with this book. To feel at home with their own abilities. To feel confident enough to be a great host. A host who revels in creativity and all the flaws that make it real. So read on, enjoy, keep it simple, eat well, and celebrate often.

KATIE BROWN

ENTERTAINS

The Rockwell Life

A LUNCH BEHIND THE FARM STAND

MENU

Grilled Vegetable Sandwich
    with a Pesto Mayo
Grilled Corn on the Cob in Husks
Fresh Tomato Salad
Blueberry Cobbler with a Cornmeal Crust

PROJECTS

Fields of Green RUNNERS AND PLACE MATS
Artichoke Easel PLACE CARDS
Ring Around the Candle LIGHTING
Got Milk GLASSES
Veggies in the Net FAVORS
Stripes TABLE

i am a total sucker for farm stands. the fact that i already

may have a bushel of pears in the back of my car or that I know I'm not going to be home for more than a week never stops me. Whenever I am driving—short trips or long—I always look for shortcuts. Backroads and country roads are my favorites; only problem is . . . for me it's never really a shortcut, 'cause I'm always stopping.

"Herb's Veggies," "Ray's Farm Goods," "Alice's Stand" . . . you name it, and I'll stop. Drive by yourself and there I'll be, loading up the car with whatever looks good that day.

I'll never forget one experience I had a few years ago, though. I was doing my usual thing. Pickin' through this barrel, siftin' through that bushel, when I realized there was nobody there. Usually there's a friendly "Can I get that for you?" or "Lemme put that in a bag for you" or "You from around here?"

But there was nobody; Frank and Mabel's Picked Right Here was silent.

I called out and nothing. I've got to admit, for a fraction of a second I thought about just taking my stuff and leaving—but that's not what it's all about at farm stands. I began to take out some money to leave somewhere, when I heard a rustle. Where was it coming from? There were voices coming from . . . hmm.

I peeked around back and then I saw it. Right out of a Rockwell painting or something. There they were—the oldest two I assumed were Frank and Mabel, with their entire family, eating corn on the cob, grilled vegetables, and other fruits of their labor. All the men had plaid shirts, and Frank even had a pipe. The table backed up to a shed and there was farm equipment scattered all over. They all had rosy cheeks and huge smiles. This was impossible; this was totally wholesome; this was *Saturday Evening Post* material!

I backed up and tiptoed back around into the stand so I didn't disturb them. I left my money on a table and drove away. I have never forgotten that lunch at the farm stand.

Fields of Green

You Need

SUPPLIES
Plywood
Sawhorses
Sod
Fresh veggies

TOOLS
Serrated knife

Sod wasn't always used for place mats and football fields. How 'bout this: sod houses! From the early days of the American pioneers' westward expansion through the early twentieth century, sod houses ("soddies") were a way of life. Examples can still be found in Nebraska and Minnesota.

Get Started

TABLE
Center plywood on two sawhorses.

RUNNER
1. Using the serrated knife, cut three 1½ × 1-foot pieces of sod and place them down the center of the plywood, leaving a space between each piece.
2. Fill the empty space between the sod pieces with a collection of fresh veggies so that the center of the table alternates between grass squares and veggie squares.

PLACE MATS
Place a 1½ × 1-foot piece of sod as place mats centered in front of each chair.

Hints and Clues
Please note the size of your sod pieces will depend upon the size of your plywood. Just make sure that you can get a checkered pattern down the center and that your place mats meet your checkerboard runner.

When your party is over it is a good idea to use the sod to cover patches in your yard.

Artichoke Easel

Get Started

1. Cut the stem of the artichokes so that the bottoms are flat and they stand up straight.
2. Trace the outline of your gift tag over the part of the photocopied snapshots that you want to use as your place card and cut out the pictures.
3. Adhere the photocopies to the gift tags with the glue stick.
4. Place a picture in between the leaves of an artichoke.

Hints and Clues

It can be fun to use funny photos because they are great conversation pieces and ice breakers.

Depending on your table decorations, photocopying all your photos in black and white can add a touch of sophistication.

You Need

SUPPLIES

Artichokes

Small gift tags

Photocopied snapshots of
   your guests' faces

TOOLS

Knife

Scissors

Glue stick

Artichokes grow on stalks, which are cut about one inch below the bottom of the fruit. From the bottom up, an artichoke is split into three main parts, the heart (the sweetest), the choke (the most bitter), and the leaves. Only the bottoms of the leaves and the heart itself are edible.

Ring Around the Candle

You Need

SUPPLIES
Rubber bands

Pillar candles

Fresh tall veggies (i.e., green beans, asparagus)

Rope

TOOLS
Scissors

Get Started

1. Pull a rubber band around the center of a candle.

2. Slide the vegetables in between the rubber band and the candle.

3. Continue adding vegetables around the circumference of the candle.

4. Tie the rope in a knot over the rubber band.

Hints and Clues

You might want to trim your veggies so they line up well.

Got Milk

SUPPLIES

Old milk bottles

Lemonade or Lipton Cold
    Brew

Simple syrup

Milk bottle tops

If you are interested in collecting milk bottles, look for bottles with the names of the dairy farms printed right on the glass in color. The permanent imprints allowed the deliverymen to know where to return the bottles. Newer milk bottles do not have the dairy names on them, and if they do, they are usually on removable labels. Another way to tell if a milk bottle is truly an antique is by looking at the top of the bottle; if there is a ridge on the inside it's old; if there is a ridge on the outside, it's new.

Get Started

1. Fill old milk bottles with fresh lemonade and lemons, or Lipton Cold Brew and simple syrup.
2. Cover with tops.

Veggies in the Net

You Need

SUPPLIES

Rope mesh bags
Vegetables from the
table runner

*The best time of year was
when we went to my aunts
and uncles for dinner and left
with pockets full of Brown
family-grown tomatoes!*

Get Started

1. Place empty mesh bags on the back of each chair.

2. When you finish the meal, share the crops on the table by telling your guests to enjoy
the fruits of the farmer's labors in their own home.

Hints and Clues

Remind your guests that they can use their bags for errands and groceries
instead of plastic!

Look for mesh bags at your local farmer's market or grocery store.

Stripes

Get Started

1. Spray-paint the table legs bright white.

2. Allow the paint to dry fully.

3. Wrap painter's tape around each leg every two inches, creating stripes.

4. Spray-paint the legs green.

5. Allow the paint to dry fully.

6. Peel off the tape.

7. Touch up with a paintbrush by spraying the paint into the paper cup and then applying with the brush.

You Need

SUPPLIES

White spray paint

Table that needs a facelift

Painter's tape

Green spray paint

TOOLS

Ruler

Paintbrush

Paper cup

Did you know that the preparation of both mayonnaise and pesto requires no cooking?

Did you know that mozzarella used to be made only from buffalo milk? Hence buffalo mozzarella.

Grilled Vegetable Sandwich with a Pesto Mayo

You Need

INGREDIENTS	AMOUNTS
Zucchini	4, sliced in ¼-inch-thick strips
Yellow squashes	4, sliced in rounds
Red onions	4, sliced in ½-inch strips
Red peppers	3, sliced in 1-inch-wide strips
Eggplants	2 large, sliced into ¼-inch-thick strips
Olive oil	6 tablespoons
Salt and pepper to taste	

PESTO MAYO

Mayonnaise	¾–1 cup
Prepared pesto	8 ounces
Sliced mozzarella	16 thin slices
Italian or thick white bread	16 slices

Get Cookin'

1. Heat grill.
2. Slice all the vegetables, brush with oil, and season with salt and pepper before placing on grill.
3. Grill until vegetables are soft and have grill marks.
4. Combine the mayonnaise and pesto to make pesto mayo.
5. Brush the bread slices with olive oil and grill till toasted.
6. Assemble sandwiches with mozzarella, vegetables, and pesto mayo.

Hints and Clues

Be sure grill is hot and clean for grilling the vegetables.

Coat your vegetables well with oil, even oil them while on the grill so they get good color and don't stick.

If you don't have a grill—or don't wish to use it—you can broil your vegetables in the oven using basically the same method.

Grilled Corn on the Cob in Husks

You Need

INGREDIENTS	AMOUNTS
Fresh sweet corn	16 ears
Salt and pepper to taste	

HERB BUTTER

Butter	1 stick (8 tablespoons), softened
Parsley	⅓ cup, finely chopped
Lemon juice	1 tablespoon

Get Cookin'

1. Remove all but the innermost layer of the husk from each ear of corn.
2. Snip off any long silk ends.
3. Grill corn, turning ears every 1 to 2 minutes, until the kernels leave dark outlines on the husks and the husks are charred, 8 to 10 minutes.
4. Remove corn from the grill, and discard the husks and silk. Arrange corn on a platter, and season with salt and pepper.
5. Serve with herb butter.

HERB BUTTER

6. Place the softened butter and parsley in a blender with lemon juice.
7. Blend until the butter is incorporated with the parsley.
8. Remove from processor, place in a heap on a piece of wax paper, and fold the paper over.
9. Use a ruler or straightedge to pull back on the paper and make a log shape with the butter.
10. Place in the refrigerator and allow to harden.
11. Remove from the refrigerator and place on a butter dish.

Hints and Clues

Be sure corn is sweet and fresh for best flavor.

Fresh Tomato Salad

You Need

INGREDIENTS	AMOUNTS
Tomatoes	7–8 medium-size, a mixture of yellow and red
Basil	1 bunch
Olive oil	1–2 tablespoons
Red wine vinegar	1 tablespoon
Salt and pepper to taste	

Get Cookin'

1. Arrange the sliced tomatoes on a large platter and place a basil leaf between each slice.
2. Drizzle with olive oil and vinegar, season with salt and pepper, and serve.

Hints and Clues

You can also combine with mozzarella or red onion, or sprinkle herbs of choice with the tomatoes.

There is very little difference in the taste of different-colored raw tomatoes. The differences are usually only in acidity, which makes some types of tomatoes better for cooking than others.

Blueberry Cobbler with a Cornmeal Crust

You Need

INGREDIENTS	AMOUNTS
CRUST	
Flour	1 cup
Cornmeal	2½ cups
Sugar	1¼ cups
Baking powder	6 teaspoons
Salt	pinch (½ teaspoon)
Buttermilk	1¼ cups
Butter	12 tablespoons, melted and cooled
Eggs	2, lightly beaten
FILLING	
Blueberries	6 cups, washed and picked
Sugar	¾ cup
Lemon juice	½ lemon
Nutmeg	½ teaspoon
Cinnamon	½ teaspoon

Get Cookin'

1. Preheat oven to 425°F.
2. Put the dry ingredients for the crust in a large bowl and whisk together.
3. Make a well in the center of the bowl of dry ingredients.
4. Add the buttermilk, butter, and eggs, combining till batter comes together.
5. In a bowl, toss the blueberries with the sugar, lemon juice, nutmeg, and cinnamon and put the mixture into a baking dish
6. Dollop the batter by spoonfuls around the edges of the dish.
7. Bake for 45 minutes or until the dough is golden brown and the berries are bubbling. Serve warm with clabbered cream or ice cream.

2

Airborne

INDUSTRIAL CHIC TAKES OFF

PROJECTS

Tack to It! PLACE MATS AND COASTERS

Metal Approach TABLE

Pushing Tin LIGHTING

Misty Marbles CENTERPIECE

Clipped PLACE CARDS

Napkins in the Pipe NAPKIN RINGS

Fans of Copper MENU

Egg Seats CHAIRS

MENU

Scallops with Ginger-Scallion Sauce

Rice and Currants

Mustard Greens Sautéed

with Water Chestnuts

Coconut Cookies

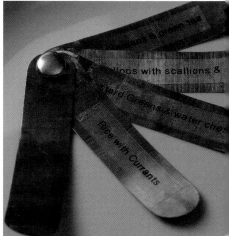

when i was a kid, i went through a stage where i was

fascinated with airplane hangars. When my friends were finished with dolls and finding out about clothes, I got a little into aviation. Sound strange? It's not quite as strange as you might think if you knew my family.

Both my parents have a pilot's license. We used to fly everywhere. It was the best way to get around. Michigan's a pretty big state and we all did a lot of things all over the place. My father was on the Board of Regents of the University of Michigan for many years (Ann Arbor wasn't exactly next to my hometown either), and he always wanted to make it home for dinner. My sisters and I all trained for ski racing and we had to be up in Lake Placid or Vermont on weekends, yet Mom wouldn't let us miss a day of school and fly. So . . . why not just have our parents fly us?

Cheaper anyway. My parents had bought a little old plane that seated six. It seemed to me

as if we spent a lot more time in the hangar than in the air. We would arrive at the airport, and Max, the man who took care of the engine in exchange for flight time, would always have something new in the engine to show my dad. They would spend a lot of time under the flap-top hood on one side or another. So, I used to wander around the hangar. As long as I wasn't complaining I could do what I wanted!

I was totally fascinated. Everywhere I looked there was metal, tools, and best of all, whole pieces of planes. Large pieces of metal riveted together with big grommets! There were two huge propellers leaning against the back wall. Everything was steel and tin, bright and shiny or old and covered with wind and age—no paint on these parts; everything had a raw, industrial look to it. Cool, cool, cool!

I'm not sure I exactly wanted to be Amelia Earhart or anything—I didn't have to be. I just loved that hangar and hanging out in there. So while my friends were in that stage between full-fledged teenagers and little girls, I was thrilled to have a place where I felt I belonged. Sometimes Max would let me bring things home. Bit by bit my shelves became a collection of aluminum, steel, and parts of old instruments. Little did I know that soon the airplane hangar would give way to the phone, dates, and movies and that my airplane parts collection would soon be replaced with posters, corsages, sparkles, and awards. This table is a small tribute to those couple of years when my parents thought I might be happy in that hangar forever and where my world was airborne and steel.

Tack to It!

You Need

SUPPLIES
Sheet metal (thin piece)
Cork plant liners
Large ones for place mats
Small ones for coasters
Silver-colored flat-headed
thumbtacks

TOOLS
Marker
Hammer
Clippers

*There must be some-
thing about coasters . . .
When I went out to buy
for GOAT, I would pick
up tons of different
coasters: vintage, hand-
made, whatever I could
find that looked good.
However, I just couldn't
keep any in stock.
People love to give and
get coasters—no matter
what they looked like,
people would just grab
them off the shelves.*

Get Started

PLACE MATS

1. Trace the shape and size of the big plant liners onto the piece of sheet metal with a marker.
2. Cut out the metal circles.
3. Tack the metal circles to the cork liners using a hammer, attaching the tacks one right after another around the circumference of the circle.
4. Line the side with another row of tacks so no cork or board is showing.

COASTERS

Pound in the tacks over the entire surface of the small cork plant liners, using a circular pattern that starts at the outside of the edge of the liners and works inward.

Metal Approach

Get Started

TABLETOP

1. Paint one side of the plywood and allow the paint to dry fully.

2. Balance the tabletop, painted side facing up, on two upside-down trash cans.

3. Pull air conditioner filters apart, saving only the metal portions.

4. Lay the metal pieces out on your table, forming a patchwork pattern (you may have to cut some in half or in thirds to make the design).

5. Connect the metal pieces where they meet with copper garden tape.

6. Place garden tape all around the 4 edges of your table. (Think of it as the frame surrounding all four sides.)

7. Nail the metal door jambs into the side edges of the plywood. (You will have to cut and trim the metal jambs to get them to your desired lengths.)

Hints and Clues

Don't worry if the table looks low;
it's meant to be!
Don't forget to wear your work gloves
while creating this project.

You Need

SUPPLIES

Plywood

High-gloss black paint

Two medium-size aluminum trash cans

Air conditioner filters (different sizes and shapes)

Metal door jambs

Copper foil garden tape ("snail tape")

TOOLS

Work gloves

Paintbrush

Clippers

Nails

Hammer

Keep your eye out for copper tape in gardening supply stores—it's used in lots of gardens and called "snail tape" because snails won't cross copper. It's a good way to keep them off your table too!

Pushing Tin

You Need

SUPPLIES
Wall patch kits
Glass votive holders
White votive candles

TOOLS
Work gloves

It's a good idea to keep a whole bunch of tea lights and votives in your closet. They're inexpensive and elegant, and you can use them just about any time and just about any place to add a lot of sparkle for a little money!

Get Started

1. Wearing the gloves, separate the metal patches.
2. Put the patch on a flat surface, sticky side up.
3. Place votive holder in the center of the patch.
4. Press down until the glass sticks to the patch.
5. Pinch corners and fold them up to form an open sack around the votive.

Misty Marbles

You Need

SUPPLIES

Tall, clear glass vases

Clear glass marbles

Keep your eye out for old marbles in antique or thrift stores. Many older marbles are worth a lot of money in the marble trade . . . you just may pick a lucky one!

Get Started

1. Fill the vases with marbles, each at different levels.

2. Fill vases with water until almost full, about 1 inch from the top.

3. Place vases down the center of the table.

Clipped

You Need

SUPPLIES

Photocopies of silverware
(3 x 2 inches)
Laminate paper
Circular nuts
(2-inch diameter)
Plumber's epoxy
Alligator clips

TOOLS

Sharpie

Get Started

1. Put two photocopies back to back. Laminate the photocopies together.

2. Fill in the centers of the nuts with plumber's epoxy. This is best done on something like foil or plastic wrap so that the epoxy doesn't bond with the work surface.

3. Place an alligator clip in the center of each nut before the epoxy dries, with the clip facing up. Allow the epoxy 24 hours to set and harden.

4. Using a Sharpie, write a guest's name on each laminated silverware photo. Place a photo in each clip.

Napkins in the Pipe

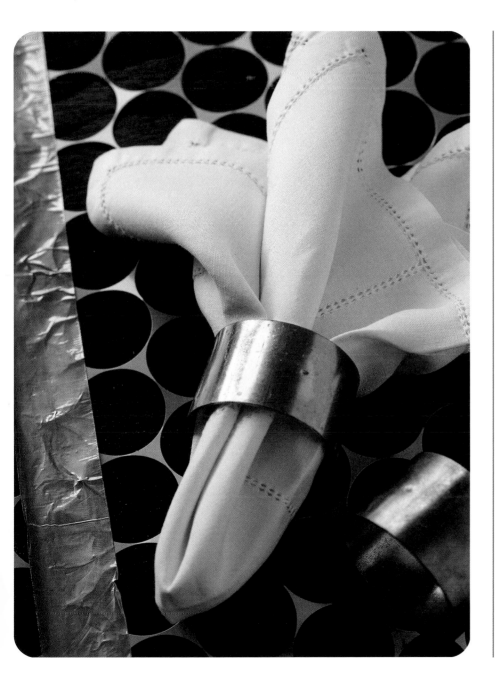

You Need

SUPPLIES

Napkins

2-inch copper piping rings

Get Started

Insert napkins through pieces
of copper pipe.

Hints and Clues

We used copper pipes because
we like the way they age, but
any type of pipe will do.

Fans of Copper

You Need

SUPPLIES
Copper garden tags
Brass brads

TOOLS
Hole punch
Label printer with clear tape

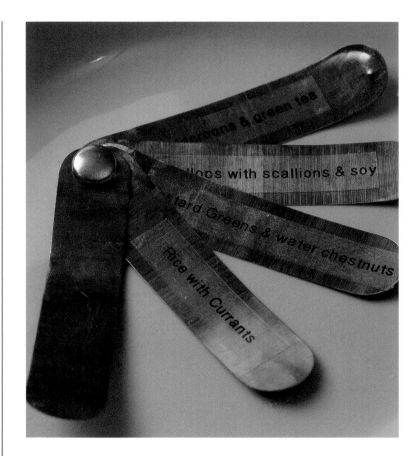

Get Started

1. Punch a hole at the end of each of the copper garden tags.
2. Print out a label for each item on the menu.
3. Place a label on each tag, except for cover tag.
4. Connect each menu by putting a brass brad through the holes of the tags.

Hints and Clues

Make sure to have as many garden tags as you do items on your menu plus one.

You may want to trim the excess flaps of the brad with scissors.

Egg Seats

You Need

SUPPLIES

White vinyl
(cut large enough to wrap
around peanut bag)
Packing peanuts

Hints and Clues

(Each chair uses 2 cubic feet.
Packing peanuts usually
come in prepackaged
containers in this amount
so just wrap up the pre-
packaged plastic bags.)

*Look for packing peanuts
made from postconsumer
materials (i.e., recycled) and
make sure they are not made
from pure Styrofoam.*

Get Started

1. Lay a vinyl piece out flat on the floor.
2. Place a bag of packing peanuts in the center of the vinyl piece and pull opposite corners of vinyl over the top of the bag of packing peanuts, tying the corners together in tight knot.
3. Repeat tying process with last two corners, making sure to tie the second knot on top of the first knot.
4. Place chairs at appropriate places.

Scallops with Ginger-Scallion Sauce

You Need

INGREDIENTS	AMOUNTS
Garlic	2 cloves, minced
Scallions	3, thinly sliced all the way up
Sugar	2 tablespoons
Soy sauce	3 tablespoons
Olive oil	2½ tablespoons (1½ for searing, 1 for sauce)
Lime juice	2 tablespoons
Water	2 tablespoons
Ginger	1 tablespoon, grated
Pepper	¼ teaspoon
Scallops	8 per person
Salt and pepper to taste	

Get Cookin'

1. Mix the sauce ingredients with a whisk in a saucepan.
2. Bring sauce to a simmer and set aside.
3. In a medium sauté pan, heat 1½ tablespoons olive oil.
4. While heating, season the scallops with salt and pepper.
5. When pan is just starting to smoke, add the scallops and sear approximately 2 to 3 minutes per side. You want a golden sear on the outside, so try not to move them around much in the pan while they are searing.
6. Remove scallops from heat.
7. Drizzle the sauce on each plate and place scallops on top.

Hints and Clues

Make sure your pan is hot before you put the scallops in for a good sear!

If you want your scallops to be cooked past medium rare, place them in the pan in a 350°F oven for about 3 minutes after they are seared.

Watch out for bright white scallops. The natural color of a raw scallop is off-white to pink. If they are white, they are saturated with water and you don't want that.

Rice and Currants

You Need

INGREDIENTS	AMOUNTS
Low-sodium chicken stock	2½ cups
White rice	1 cup
Dried currants	½ cup
Salt	½ teaspoon
Pepper	a pinch

Get Cookin'

1. Bring the stock to a boil.
2. Add the rice and dried currants to the stock and cover saucepan. Lower temperature to a simmer and cook for 20 minutes, or until liquid is absorbed and rice is cooked. Remove pan from heat.
3. Fluff rice with a fork and season with the salt and pepper.

Did you know that currants were originally found in Corinth, Greece . . . that's where they got their names! Corinth (be)gat currant!

Mustard Greens Sautéed with Water Chestnuts

You Need

INGREDIENTS	AMOUNTS
Olive oil	3 tablespoons
Shallots	2 teaspoons, minced
Garlic	2 cloves, thinly sliced
Water chestnuts	½ cup, thinly sliced
Mustard greens	2 pounds, washed, dried, and torn into pieces
Water	2 tablespoons
Lemon juice	1½ tablespoons
Salt and pepper to taste	

Get Cookin'

1. In a large sauté pan, heat the olive oil over medium heat and add the shallots and garlic. Sauté for about 1 minute.
2. Add the water chestnuts and cook for about 1 minute.
3. Add the mustard greens and toss until they are wilted, about 1 minute.
4. Add water and lemon juice and season with salt and pepper to taste.

Hints and Clues

Kale can be substituted for mustard greens in this recipe.

If you like mustard greens, try kale or collard greens. Often used in soul food, mustard greens and collard greens are often ignored in other cooking, and they're pretty tasty!

Coconut Cookies

You Need

INGREDIENTS	AMOUNTS
Egg whites	3 large eggs
Salt	pinch
Granulated sugar	⅓ cup
Shredded coconut	1½ cups
Light brown sugar	⅓ cup
Pure vanilla extract	1 teaspoon
All-purpose flour	1 teaspoon

Get Cookin'

1. Preheat oven to 325°F.
2. Lightly butter a cookie sheet and line with parchment paper.
3. In a very clean, dry mixing bowl with a clean whisk (free of grease or whites will deflate), mix the egg whites. Start on a slow speed until they bubble and then increase to medium speed.
4. Add salt to the whites and increase speed until soft fluffy peaks form.
5. Add 1 tablespoon of the granulated sugar and mix the whites for about 2 minutes until thick and glossy (think of Marshmallow Fluff).
6. In a separate bowl, combine the coconut, remaining granulated sugar, brown sugar, and vanilla extract. Mix well with your hands, making sure to crumble all the brown sugar so that the mixture is even.
7. Take a scoop of the egg white mixture and add it to the coconut mixture. With a spatula, gently mix by folding as if you are taking a paddle and inserting it into the center of the mixture, then scooping up and out. Do this gently.
8. Add the mixture to the remaining egg whites, and continue folding.
9. Drop the mixture by heaping teaspoons onto the prepared cookie sheet and bake for 12–15 minutes until golden.
10. Set aside to cool for a minute until the bottom is slightly sticky but with care you can gently lift the cookies off the pan. Transfer them to a cooling rack. Let cool and serve.
11. The final texture should be soft and chewy.

3

Lone Star

A FOURTH OF JULY CELEBRATION

MENU

Chili-Rubbed Flank Steak

Lone Star Coleslaw

Skillet Corn Bread
            with Jalapeño and Pecans

Red, White, and Blue Almond Shortcakes

PROJECTS

The Patriots NAPKIN RINGS

Branded and Seared PLACE MATS

Rin Tin Tin GLASSES

Ticking-Tac-Toe CHAIRS

Cactus Roundup CENTERPIECE

Hide and Stud TABLETOP

i'll never forget driving across Texas. i stayed much too long,

but I couldn't help myself. I loved everything about it. I drove down long roads that I'm sure every restaurant I passed was "All you can eat, all night long" . . . and I did!

I met strangers who became friends, and discovered a way of life that I can't forget. The Texans I met somehow managed to be bold, brassy, and down-to-earth all at the same time. I went to backyard barbecues with beauty queens. I ate dinners with ranchers who tipped their ten-gallon hats every time a lady passed by.

With each mile I drove, I became completely wrapped up in Texas style. I don't know

exactly what it was: the vastness of the open land I drove across, the people, the food, or the style. Whatever it was, it worked. For me, Texas embodies an American spirit that cannot be duplicated in any other country. I love it all—the boots, the oil wells, the mesquite flavor in the air, and the pride of the people.

Everywhere I went I learned a little more about Texas history. Not stuff I learned about in school, either. Texans love the nitty-gritty of their history. I found out that Sam Houston was brought up by Indians, married three times, and was scared of nothing. I can tell you lots about the Alamo—I feel like I remember it myself. I am also thoroughly convinced that if Texas had not joined the states, America may not have been successful in its westward

expansion. I was totally amazed at how aware and secure each and every Texan is about their role in American history.

When we started writing this book, I really wanted to include a Fourth of July chapter. Growing up, the Fourth of July was always a time my family spent together, and it remains a special summer celebration to me. After a recent return to Texas, there was not a question in my mind that the Independence Day celebration would be Lone Star style. It had to be big, bold, and totally American. In a word—Texan. Could there be a better way to celebrate America? Hay, leather, and red, white, and blue. What could be more simple and more like the U.S.A.?

The Patriots

You Need

SUPPLIES

Napkins
Small (4 x 6 inches)
American flags
1-foot leather shoelace strips

TOOLS

Scissors

> *Did you know that the American flag flies over the White House only when the President is in residence?*

Get Started

1. Roll each napkin lengthwise, giving them a sturdy, baton-like feel.

2. Wrap flags around each rolled-up napkin. Keep the stripes vertical.

3. Tie a piece of leather shoelace around the center of each flag.

4. Tie the two tails off in knots to give the ring a finished look.

Hints and Clues

If you can't find small flags, use small flags on sticks. Simply remove the flags from the sticks for use.

You may have to trim each flag to better show off both stars and stripes.

Branded and Seared

Get Started

1. Write your guests' names 2 to 4 inches from the top of the place mat with your wood burnishing tools.
2. Hammer a nail halfway into the wood in each of the four corners.
3. Tie off one end of your leather shoestring to the upper left nail, then wrap the length of the additional strip around the perimeter, wrapping around each nail head once.
Continue this process around the place mat until you reach the upper left nail head again and tie off. Trim with scissors. Remember to leave a bit of length after you have tied off the final corner — it's fun in a rawhide sort of way.
4. Place a dab of hot glue on the nail head of the upper left nail and press on your precut wooden star.

Hints and Clues

If you have different sizes of plywood cut into squares lying around, don't be afraid to use them as place mats. Mix and match/big and small, it's a great way to make scraps of wood useful.

If you want to make it more like a ranch and less like a place card, use your initials and burnish them into your place mats. If your home has a name, write that out, e.g., Ponderosa.

You Need

SUPPLIES
13 x 18 inch pieces of plywood
1-inch roofing nails
Leather shoestrings
1-inch wooden stars

TOOLS
Wood burnishing tool and tip
Hammer
Scissors
Glue gun and glue sticks

Rin Tin Tin

You Need

SUPPLIES

2½ to 3 yards vinyl leather

Tin cans

Leather shoestring

TOOLS

Scissors

Awl

Embroidery needle

Get Started

1. Cut a piece of leather, enough to cover the circumference of the tin can, leaving an extra inch on the top and bottom and leaving an extra ¼ inch where the seams join.

2. Fold a 1-inch border along one length of leather, creating a smooth edge.

3. Puncture holes approximately ½ inch apart along the entire length using the awl.

4. Repeat this process along the opposite edge as well as along the width seams.

5. Thread your needle with a leather shoestring.

6. Whipstitch the hems at the top and bottom.

7. Join the seams by whipstitching them to create the sleeve. (This is a good time to test your desired width. Remember, you don't want the sleeve to be too tight or too loose, but just right. We found it's best to leave these ends untied until you have placed the sleeve on the can; that way you can adjust accordingly.)

8. Place a glass inside the can.

Hints and Clues

Collect tin cans that fit your glasses of choice. We chose a medium-size soup can to fit our pint glasses.

Remember to carefully fold or bend any sharp edges on a can with pliers—this will make it easier and a bit safer to clean them.

Ticking-Tac-Toe

You Need

SUPPLIES

Bed pillows, preferably firm

1 yard mattress ticking

Thin gauge silver wire

TOOLS

Upholstery needle

Scissors

Get Started

1. Wrap a pillow with mattress ticking, leaving excess trim as you would when wrapping a gift to create neat folds.

2. Thread the needle with the thin gauge wire.

3. Visualize the face of the pillow as a grid. Create the checkerboard pattern by piercing each section with a piece of wire and pulling it through the fabric, through the pillow, and out the other side. Pull it taut and tie off in a knot, creating a tufted surface.

4. Roll the ends inward on both sides, until the roll meets the pillow.

5. Secure the ends with wire. Make sure you place the wire on the roll along the same lines as the other wires in the grid, therefore continuing the checkerboard pattern.

6. Put pillows on the ground around the table as seats.

Hints and Clues

This is a great way to make use out of old pillows!

When you are working with the wire you may want to wear protective gloves.

Did you know that new American mattresses are rarely wrapped in "mattress ticking," but the ticking stripe and fabric are staples in any fabric and craft store today. It's durable, strong, and it looks great.

Cactus Roundup

You Need

SUPPLIES
Dried bunches of wheat

Various sizes
of terra-cotta pots

36-inch leather shoestrings

Cacti

Potting soil

TOOLS
Hot glue gun

Shears

Thick gloves

Did you know that many cacti are edible? In fact, in Texas a cactus salad might be listed on any menu!

Get Started

PREPARING THE POTS

1. Cut wheat stalks to measure 1 to 2 inches above the lip of the terra-cotta pots.
2. Hot glue the wheat stalks all the way around the pots.
3. Trim the uneven edges along the top and bottom with shears.
4. Wrap a leather shoestring 2 to 3 times around each wheat-covered pot and tie to secure, leaving 2-inch tails.
5. Tie finishing knots at the end of the tails.

POTTING THE CACTI

6. Put the cacti in the wheat-wrapped pots. Wear gloves!
7. Add soil and water. (Remember to allow for proper drainage.)
8. Place potted cacti down the center of the table.

Hints and Clues
We used all different varieties of cacti for texture!

Hide and Stud

You Need

SUPPLIES

Hollow unfinished
   3 x 8-foot door
3½ x 8½-foot piece
   of brown pleather
1-inch roofing nails

TOOLS

Staple gun
Hammer
Scissors or shears

Get Started

TABLE LEGS

1. Cover the cinder blocks with hay by wrapping the hay around the blocks and securing it with wire.

2. Put the blocks in place.

3. Slip an American flag vertically between the hay and a couple of the wire wraps to help secure it. (Don't forget to make sure the flag faces outward.)

4. Cover the wire by wrapping it with rope and tying a big knot in front.

TABLETOP

1. Cover the door with the vinyl fabric and staple it to the underside.

2. Hammer roofing nails every 4 to 6 inches around the perimeter of your tabletop.

3. Place tabletop on cinder block legs.

Hints and Clues

We used roofing nails because they are big and round and give the table a western feel.

Did you know that the triangular formation that an American flag is folded in is meant to resemble the founding fathers' tricorner hats?

Did you know that Christopher Columbus brought the first chili pepper to Europe from the New World?

Chili-Rubbed Flank Steak

You Need

INGREDIENTS	AMOUNTS
Garlic	5 cloves
Cumin	½ teaspoon
Cilantro	¼ cup
Red chipotle chilis	7-ounce can, just the chilis
Olive oil	2 tablespoons
Salt	1 teaspoon
Pepper	1 teaspoon
Flank steak	4 pounds (½ pound per person)

Get Cookin'

MAKING THE RUB

1. Place the garlic, cumin, and cilantro in food processor and blend until roughly chopped.
2. Add the chilis, olive oil, salt, and pepper and process until they are smooth.

PREPARING THE MEAT

3. Rub the chili mixture onto the flank steak. Let steak sit in refrigerator overnight or stand at room temperature 2 to 3 hours. (If you refrigerate, allow the meat to come to room temperature before grilling.)
4. Grill over hot flame for about 5 minutes per side for medium rare.

Hints and Clues

Use a spoon or spatula to put on the rub to avoid getting the spicy rub all over your hands.

You can substitute canned jalapeños or other red chilis if chipotles are not available.

Lone Star Coleslaw

....

You Need

INGREDIENTS	AMOUNTS
Preshredded cabbage for coleslaw	4 cups
Carrots	3, peeled and shredded
Radishes	2 bunches, thinly sliced in rounds
Mayonnaise	1½ cups
Mustard	1 tablespoon
Apple cider vinegar	¼ cup
Sugar	⅓ cup
Tabasco sauce	½ teaspoon
Cayenne pepper	½ teaspoon
Salt and pepper to taste	

Get Cookin'

1. Mix together the coleslaw mix, carrots, and radishes. Set aside.

2. Mix all other ingredients except the salt and pepper together in a large bowl with a whisk until smooth.

3. Add the dressing to the slaw and toss.

4. Salt and pepper to taste.

5. Refrigerate for at least 1 hour before serving.

Hints and Clues

You can make the coleslaw a day in advance. Taste and season before serving. The sweetness of the coleslaw should balance the spicy chili-rubbed flank steak and jalapeño corn bread.

The word coleslaw comes from the Dutch koolsla meaning . . . "cool cabbage"!

Corn bread is as all-American as you can get; you would be hard-pressed to find it in another country. But while you're in this one . . . the best corn bread is at Mesa Grill in New York!

Skillet Corn Bread with Jalapeño and Pecans

You Need

INGREDIENTS	AMOUNTS
Crisco	2 tablespoons
Yellow coarse ground cornmeal	2 cups
Baking powder	4 teaspoons
Sugar	⅓ cup, plus enough to sprinkle over the top
Salt	1 teaspoon
Egg	1
Buttermilk	1½ cups
Honey	½ cup
Butter	3 tablespoons, melted
Jalapeño	2 tablespoons, minced
Pecans	½ cup, roughly chopped

Get Cookin'

1. Preheat oven to 450°F.
2. Place a 9-inch cast-iron skillet with Crisco in the hot oven while you make the batter.
3. Combine cornmeal, baking powder, sugar, and salt in a mixing bowl.
4. Slowly add the egg and buttermilk to the dry ingredients, stirring just until blended.
5. Add honey.
6. Add the melted butter and then stir in the jalapeños and pecans.
7. Remove skillet from the oven and pour batter into it.
8. Sprinkle sugar on top.
9. Return to the oven and bake until the top is golden and a knife inserted in the center comes out clean, 20 to 25 minutes.

Hints and Clues

The corn bread can also be made in an 8- or 9-inch square pan.

Preheating the pan makes a real difference in the browning and crust of the bread.

You can also use boxed corn bread mix. Just add in the honey, pecans, and jalapeños.

Red, White, and Blue Almond Shortcakes

You Need

INGREDIENTS	AMOUNTS
Bisquick	3⅓ cups
Milk	¾ cup
Sugar	¼ cup, plus more for sprinkling
Butter	4 tablespoons, melted
Almond extract	2 tablespoons
Almond slices	¼ cup, plus more for sprinkling
FILLING	
Strawberries	1 pint, hulled and sliced
Blueberries	1 pint
Sugar	3 tablespoons
Lemon juice	1 lemon
Cool Whip	1½ cups

Get Cookin'

1. Preheat oven to 425°F.

2. Stir all the ingredients for the shortcakes together.

3. Turn out dough onto a lightly floured surface and knead a few times till it comes together.

4. Using a floured rolling pin, roll dough out to a 1-inch thickness and then cut out 2½-inch rounds with a cookie cutter.

5. Place cakes on an ungreased cookie sheet 1 inch apart. Sprinkle with sliced almonds and sugar. Bake for 15 minutes, or until shortcakes are golden on top and light brown on the bottom.

6. Let cool.

7. To serve, slice the shortcakes in half horizontally and spoon on a layer of cool whip and a layer of filling. Replace the top of the shortcake and finish the top with more cool whip and filling.

4

Hopscotch

A WHIMSICAL LUNCH FOR KIDS OF ALL AGES

PROJECTS

Go-Go à Ice Cream BOWLS

Seating Assignments PLACE CARDS

Puzzle-tations INVITATIONS

Big Block Box of Chalk FAVORS

Bloomin' Pinwheels CENTERPIECE

Plate Rules PLACE MATS

Face the Chalkboard TABLE

Flower Power PLATES

MENU

The Leaning Tower of Cheese

Spicy Onion Rings

Three-Bean Salad
    with Mustard-Tarragon Dressing

Brownie Sundaes
    with Creamy Butterscotch Sauce

a few weeks ago i woke up and i had one of those mornings

where I just wanted to be a kid again. You know, the kind of day where you wake up and you pull the covers up over your face, leaving just your eyes peering out—and you wait. You look back and forth, waiting for your mom to come into your room and get you out of bed. The kind of morning where you arc sure if you delay long enough you'll smell the breakfast that's cooking for you in the kitchen.

I waited.

. . . and waited

. . . and waited.

Nobody came.

There were no smells from the kitchen, either. I finally got out of bed and my clothes weren't even laid out for me. Oh well, I thought. I guess all this is not a dream . . . I'm a grown-up and I've got to get downstairs and make some coffee!

Wandering around the kitchen, I wondered just what I could do about the whole grown-up thing that day. I just didn't want to do it. It was Saturday and I had invited some friends over for lunch. My morning mood just wouldn't wear off, so I decided to have some fun with it. Why not? I crossed off just about everything on my shopping list for my luncheon that day, and went down to my local dollar mart. I wanted chalkboards, pinwheels, hopscotch, and grilled cheese on paper plates. Hopefully my friends would too . . . 'cuz that's what they were gettin'!

The lunch turned out to be pretty fun, and I didn't have to wash one plate (kids never really do!). Now whenever I feel like being a kid, I go with it! It's fun, it's festive and, well . . . it's not wrong.

Fortunately for me, my friends are used to my quirky moods and themed dinners. If you're not quite as full of whimsy (or your friends not as patient as mine), this table does make a great party for real kids. Back-to-school, birthday, or *whatever* excuse, it's all about fun!

Go-Go à Ice Cream

One of the most popular items at GOAT were martini glasses set on top of race cars. Since kids can't drink martinis, I borrowed the idea and just substituted dessert bowls for the cocktail glasses.

You Need

SUPPLIES

Clear bowls

Toy cars

Clear silicon gel

Masking or electrical tape

Get Started

1. Glue the glass bowls onto the top of the toy car with clear silicon gel.

2. Wrap tape around the car and the bowl until dry.

3. Remove tape and you have a runaway sundae!

Hints and Clues

Make sure that the toy cars have a flat top for gluing.

Seating Assignments

Get Started

1. Drill small holes into the top corners of the wood borders of each chalkboard.

2. Thread a ribbon through one side and tie it on with a knot. Allow yourself about 10 to 12 inches for hanging and tie the ribbon through the hole on the other side with a knot.

3. Trim the ends of the ribbon.

4. Write your guests' names on each chalkboard.

5. Hammer a small tack into the back of each chair and hang the chalkboard from the tack.

Hints and Clues

Mini chalkboards make great party favors!

You Need

SUPPLIES

Small chalkboards

Ribbon

Chalk

Tacks

TOOLS

Drill

Scissors

Hammer

Up until as late as the 1940s, miniature chalkboards were a part of every school-child's day. Before paper was as widely available as it is today, children used small chalkboards to learn how to write, to answer questions, and to do their homework and solve mathematical equations.

Puzzle-tations

You Need

SUPPLIES

Small cardboard puzzles

Chalkboard paint

Chalk

TOOLS

Paintbrush

Get Started

1. Separate the puzzle pieces. Don't mix up the different puzzles when painting.

2. Paint the pieces with two coats of chalkboard paint.

3. Put the puzzle back together when the paint is dry.

4. Write out the invitation with chalk.

Hints and Clues

Remember to keep each of the puzzle's pieces separate as you paint them to make reassembly easy!

Big Block Box of Chalk

Get Started

1. Have ⅛-inch-thick pieces of plywood cut to cover 4 sides and a top of the cardboard boxes. When ordering, remember that 2 sides should be ⅛ inch longer than the other 2 sides to create a finished corner. The top should be ⅛ inch bigger on all 4 sides to completely cover the box.

2. Using rubber cement, glue the 4 pieces onto the sides of the cardboard box. Wrap the box with masking tape and allow to dry.

3. Using rubber cement again, glue a lettered block onto the center of the top.

4. Repeat steps 2 and 3 for the rest of the cardboard boxes, until you have one for each quest.

5. Fill each box with chalk.

Hints and Clues

It is fun to choose block letters that start with the first letter of your guests' names.

Antique wooden toys have always been popular collectibles. When looking for older wooden blocks, always check weight and paint color. The older the block, the less likely it is to have a shiny finish. Newer blocks also tend to be smaller and lighter. The edges are usually slightly worn, but make sure there are no cracks in the wood.

You Need

SUPPLIES

⅛-inch-thick plywood precut to size

Cardboard boxes

Rubber cement

Masking tape

Lettered wooden blocks

Chalk

Bloomin' Pinwheels

You Need

SUPPLIES

Wrapping paper

Laminate paper

1-inch wire brads

2-foot-long dowels

Buttons

Various terra-cotta pots

Sugar

Jelly beans

TOOLS

Ruler

Scissors

Hammer

Masking tape

Glue gun and glue sticks

Keep your eye out for wallpaper samples in bright colors to use for pinwheels and other fun projects.

Get Started

PINWHEELS

1. Choose fun wrapping paper and cut it into squares.

2. Laminate the paper squares.

3. Cut the square diagonally from each corner into the center, leaving 1 inch uncut in the center. You will be cutting 4 times, creating 4 triangles with a 1-inch circle in the center.

4. Make a hole in the bottom right-hand corner of the triangle closest to you.

5. Turn the square clockwise and make a hole in the bottom right-hand corner of the next triangle.

6. Repeat until there is a hole in each triangle.

7. Insert the brad through one of the holes, pull the flap over, and push it through the next hole until all 4 flaps meet in the center.

8. Push the nail through the center of the square, with all 4 flaps still connected to create the final pinwheel shape.

9. Hammer the pinwheel to the top of the dowel. To prevent the dowel from splitting, place a strip of masking tape 2 inches down from the top.

10. Glue a button onto the nail head in the center of the pinwheel.

11. Glue additional buttons on the edges of the pinwheel flaps.

JELLY BEAN POTS

12. Cover the hole in the bottom of the terra-cotta pots with a thick piece of tape.

13. Fill the pots with sugar.

14. Insert the pinwheels.

15. Vary the pinwheel heights by cutting the dowels.

16. Fill the tops of the terra-cotta pots with multicolored jelly beans.

Hints and Clues

Look for interesting or vintage buttons to dress up the pinwheel!

Plate Rules

You Need

SUPPLIES

4 12-inch rulers with holes per
place mat
1 yard of ribbon per place mat

TOOLS

Hot glue gun

*Keep your eye out
for wooden rulers
and yardsticks
without metal edges.*

Get Started

1. Glue the rulers together in a rectangle or square.
2. Tie a colorful piece of ribbon around each of the four corners.

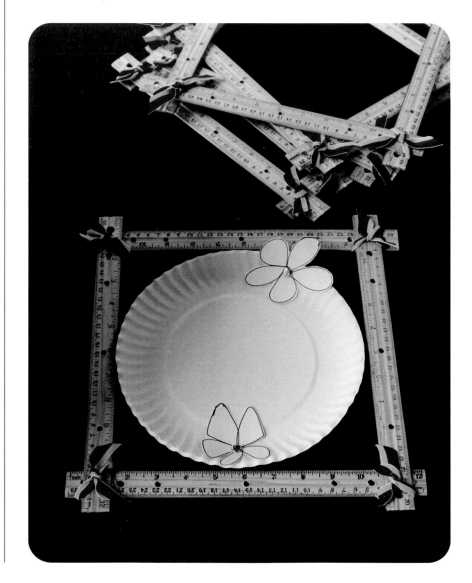

Face the Chalkboard

You Need

SUPPLIES

Plywood

Chalkboard paint

Sawhorses

Yardsticks with holes
at either end

1-inch roofing nails

TOOLS

Paintbrush

Hammer

Handsaw

Glue gun

Get Started

1. Paint one side of the plywood with 2 coats of chalkboard paint and allow to dry, then center the plywood over 2 sawhorses.

2. Hammer the yardsticks into the edge of the plywood through the holes on either end all the way around the table. If you have to cut some yardsticks down to fit, they should be hot-glued to the table edge.

Hints and Clues

Draw or write with chalk on your tabletop. A hopscotch or a rhyme or whatever you like — have fun!

The best ever were the days when your hardware store gave away wooden yardsticks with their logo printed on them.

Flower Power

You Need

SUPPLIES
Paper plates

TOOLS
Scissors

Hole punch

Brass fasteners

Get Started

1. Draw some flower patterns on the middle section of a paper plate.

2. Cut out the drawings on the outside of the lines to give the appliqué definition.

3. Make a hole in the center of the floral applique and insert a small brass fastener through the hole.

4. Make a few holes around the edge of the paper plate.

5. Attach the appliqués with the fastener.

Hints and Clues

Put as many flowers as you like on each plate.

It is fun to use color markers to draw the flowers.

The Leaning Tower of Cheese

You Need

INGREDIENTS	AMOUNTS
Cheddar cheese	8 ounces, cut in thin slices
Plum tomatoes	5, sliced in thin rounds
Mozzarella cheese	8 ounces, cut in thin slices
Hot dog rolls	16, sliced in half with tops trimmed off
Butter	6 tablespoons

Get Cookin'

1. Preheat oven to 350°F.
2. Place 2 pieces of Cheddar cheese, 2 tomato slices, and 2 slices of mozzarella cheese on the bread. Place the second piece of bread on top, creating a sandwich.
3. Heat 3 tablespoons of butter over medium heat.
4. Once heated, place the grilled cheese in the pan and allow it to cook until the bread is golden and toasted.
5. Turn the bread and fry on the other side until toasted, about 4 minutes.
6. Place the sandwiches on a baking pan and place in the oven for 5 minutes.
7. Remove from oven and slice in half on a diagonal.
8. Place 4 halves on a skewer.

Hints and Clues

We topped the skewer with a wooden block by drilling a small hole halfway through the block for a more festive look!

Grilled cheese was one of the first culinary delights I mastered . . .

Spicy Onion Rings

....

You Need

INGREDIENTS	AMOUNTS
Canola oil	4 cups
Vidalia onions	5, sliced in fat rounds
Buttermilk	1 quart
Chili sauce	½ cup
Salt	3 teaspoons
Flour	2¼ cups

Get Cookin'

1. Heat canola oil in fryer or heavy pot.
2. Whisk together the buttermilk, chili sauce, 1 teaspoon salt, and ¼ cup flour.
3. Soak the sliced onion rings in the buttermilk mixture for at least 5 minutes, making sure to thoroughly coat the rings.
4. Mix the remaining flour with 2 teaspoons salt in a flat baking dish.
5. When ready to fry, dip the rings into the baking dish with the flour mixture and place them in the fryer in batches, making sure they are not crowded.
6. When rings are golden and crispy (about 3 minutes), remove and drain on a paper towel. Salt to taste and serve.

Hints and Clues

Do not crowd the fryer because the rings will steam instead of fry and they won't have a crispy coating. Whisk the batter before dipping the onions in it. That makes the batter thicker and will help the dry flour adhere to the rings.

Always use caution when frying.

Tongs are a very useful tool for this recipe; they will make it easier to place the rings in the oil and remove them.

Three-Bean Salad with Mustard-Tarragon Dressing

You Need

INGREDIENTS	AMOUNTS
Salt	2 teaspoons
Water	2 cups
Green beans	8 ounces, ends removed and cut in 1½-inch pieces
Cannellini beans	1 can (15 ounces), drained
Kidney beans	1 can (15 ounces), drained
Red pepper	1, diced
Yellow pepper	1, diced
Shallot	1, diced

DRESSING

Red wine vinegar	¼ cup
Mustard	1 tablespoon
Honey	1 teaspoon
Fresh tarragon	2 tablespoons, chopped
Salt	¼ teaspoon
Pepper	¼ teaspoon
Canola oil	¼ cup

Salt and pepper to taste

Get Cookin'

1. Salt the water and bring to a boil.
2. Add the green beans and cook at a simmer for 5 minutes, until the beans are tender but still slightly crunchy.
3. Drain and then immediately fill saucepan with ice water. This will stop the beans from cooking and also give them a bright green color.
4. Drain the beans from the ice water and then mix together with the cannellini beans, kidney beans, diced peppers, and shallot.

5. Toss with the mustard-tarragon dressing (recipe follows) and salt and pepper to taste; serve at room temperature.

DRESSING

1. Place the red wine vinegar, mustard, honey, tarragon, salt, and pepper in a blender. Mix until ingredients are combined.

2. With the blender on, slowly pour in the oil until the dressing has emulsified or the oil has been fully incorporated into the dressing.

Hints and Clues

This salad can be made ahead of time (up to a day) and kept in the refrigerator, but it should be served at room temperature so the flavors will come out.

Don't have time to slowly add ingredients together to create an emulsion? With simple dressings, try throwing all the ingredients together in a mini food processor, turn it on for a couple of seconds and presto, you've got an emulsion! What could be easier!

Brownie Sundaes with Creamy Butterscotch Sauce

You Need

INGREDIENTS	AMOUNTS
Store-bought brownie mix	1 box
Chocolate chips	½ cup
Unsalted butter	8 tablespoons (1 stick)
Light brown sugar	⅔ cup
Granulated sugar	⅔ cup
Salt	1½ teaspoons
Water	2 tablespoons
Light corn syrup	¾ cup
Heavy cream	¾ cup
Vanilla extract	2 teaspoons
Ice cream of choice	1 gallon

Get Cookin'

1. Make brownies following package directions, but add chocolate chips to the mix.

2. In a heavy-bottomed medium saucepan, melt butter.

3. Stir in sugars, salt, water, and corn syrup.

4. Bring to a boil over medium-high heat, stirring to dissolve sugars.

5. Keep at a slow boil for 5 minutes and stir often.

6. Remove from heat and carefully whisk in the cream and vanilla extract.

7. Allow to cool before serving.

8. Cut the brownies. Place a square in the bottom of a bowl, top with a scoop of ice cream, and pour the butterscotch sauce over the top.

Hints and Clues

Butterscotch can be made ahead and brought to room temperature just before using (don't use it hot—it will completely melt the ice cream).

If you want to top your sundae with peanuts, here's how to toast them: Put unsalted cocktail nuts on a cookie sheet, place in 350°F oven, and toast for 8 to 10 minutes. When cooked, roughly chop.

5

May Day
the Old-fashioned Way

A DINNER FOR TWELVE

MENU

Ham with Garlic and Rosemary

Buttermilk Biscuits with Cheddar Cheese

Fresh Peas with Cream

Mrs. Brown's Scalloped Potatoes

Almond Apricot Tart

PROJECTS

Flowing like a Ribbon CHAIR

Hoop-La HEADDRESS

A Spring Canvas TABLECLOTH

Floral Bracelet FAVORS

Stick in the Moss CENTERPIECE

Frame Game PLACE MATS

Dream Weaver NAPKINS

have you ever seen a black-and-white photo but for some

reason you just knew what colors the people were wearing? You knew the color of their hair, you knew . . . how rare the meat on the table was? Well . . . I feel that way about all black-and-white photos. I look at them and I just KNOW exactly what everything looked like.

When I was really young, I used to look through old family photos all the time. I'd start with my parents' wedding and move backward . . . nothing after that was too much of a mystery anyway. I gotta admit, though, the wedding was a favorite for quite

a while. I began to look through my grandmother's old albums. Most of the pictures were tiny—and attached to this horrible black paper that was disintegrating and would get all over me—but I loved them. To me, the May Day pictures were the best.

When my grandmother was young, May Day was a big deal! Every year, on May first, there were parties and fun. The pictures show all the young girls braiding ribbons around the Maypole. They were all wearing white dresses and had ribbons in their hair. Everything else—I just know it—was all pastels. My grandmother's yard became a sea of white and pastels: pinks, lavenders, light greens, and yellows. There were games, flowers, and what looked to be so much fun!

I think we should bring May Day back! How fun would it be to take everybody out in your yard—or living room or wherever—and re-create a widely forgotten tradition! I think it would be the best! But if you can't manage at May Day, try Easter, Passover, or any spring day. Just have some fun with the colors and bring traditions of spring back. You might just be surprised at how fun they are. Don't have any ideas? Just look at some old pictures!

Flowing like a Ribbon

You Need

SUPPLIES

1 ½-inch-wide
grosgrain ribbon
14-inch-round paper doilies

TOOLS

Scissors

Get Started

1. Cut ribbon into lengths long enough to trail behind the chairs.

2. Place a doily on the seat of a chair.

3. String ribbons through a large opening in the doily on either side and tie each piece of ribbon around the chair back.

4. Let the ribbon tails trail off the back of the chair and drape on the floor.

Hints and Clues

Choose grosgrain, French wire, or organdy ribbon for your chair ties because they hold their shape better.

Introduce a stripe or a polka dot ribbon to add a touch of pattern to your setting.

Guest Appeal: Pack a gift when you go over to somebody's house for dinner or lunch. Nothing big . . . just something to say Thanks, I'll be back!

Hoop-La

Get Started

1. Cut 2 pieces of grosgrain ribbon each the length of the circumference of the hoop, adding an inch at the end.

2. Sandwich the hoop between the 2 pieces of ribbon.

3. Glue the 2 ribbons together at the edges, an inch at a time, all the way around the hoop.

4. Seal at the ends with glue and cut off any excess ribbon.

5. Repeat process for each hoop.

6. Cut 4 pieces of fishing line that are long enough to hang the hoops from the ceiling so that the bottom hoop is at an appropriate height above the table. Remember . . . you'll need a few extra inches to secure the hoops to one another.

7. Tie the 4 pieces of fishing line around the largest hoop at equidistant points.

8. Connect the middle-size hoop by bringing the 4 pieces of line up and wrapping them around the hoop at an appropriate height.

9. Repeat the process to attach the top (smallest) hoop.

10. Gather the 4 lines above the topmost hoop and hang the hoop assembly from the ceiling.

11. Cut 4 pieces of sheer organdy ribbon. The ribbons should be long enough to flow from the ceiling, down to the table and outward to the edges to drape to the floor.

12. Tie each piece of ribbon to the top of each piece of the fishing lines as close to the ceiling as possible and follow each fishing line with the ribbon, wrapping each ribbon around the hoop once where the line is tied. Leave each ribbon to trail on to the table, and from there to the floor.

Hints and Clues

We found the best way to get the ribbon tails to stay where we wanted them was to attach them to the four corners of the table with Velcro.

You Need

SUPPLIES

1½-inch-wide
    grosgrain ribbon
One 36-inch needlework hoop
One 24-inch needlework hoop
One 18-inch needlework hoop
Fishing line
1½-inch-wide sheer
    organdy ribbon

TOOLS

Hot glue gun
Scissors

A Spring Canvas

You Need

SUPPLIES

Canvas (large enough
for use as a tablecloth)
Matte board
White high-gloss paint
Yellow high-gloss paint

TOOLS

Pencil
Ruler
Handsaw
Paintbrush

Get Started

1. Sketch diamond pattern on the canvas with pencil and ruler, creating a Harlequin design.
2. Cut a diamond out of the matte board the size of the diamonds already sketched.
3. Place the template over the diamond that will be your starting point and paint with one color.
4. Continue by filling in every other diamond with some paint color.
5. Let dry.
6. Use template to fill in remaining diamonds with second color.
7. Let dry.

Hints and Clues

It's easy to go off course when you are filling in the diamonds with paint. We found it was a good idea to mark the diamonds intended for alternate color with tape.

Try to dab the paint through the stencil, rather than brushing it over the edges, so that it stays in its boundaries.

After my first semester of college, I brought home a painting on a large piece of canvas. It was the only thing I had to show as a product of my intended major. My parents took it from me and hung it at the top of the staircase. Each time my parents had guests over, for several years after, they would motion to the painting and refer to it as "our dividend."

Floral Bracelet

One of the reasons I love wrist corsages is because, when I was of-the-prom age, my mom always made me carry nosegays. My date would call and ask what kind of dress I was wearing so he could get me a matching wrist corsage, but I had to tell him I wanted a nosegay! For years, while all of my friends were wearing corsages, I had to carry around little bouquets. I was embarrassed. So now . . . wrist corsages for all!

You Need

SUPPLIES
Wide ribbon
Single flowers
Floral tape
Mason jars
Packing tags

TOOLS
Scissors
Sharpie

Get Started

1. Cut a length of ribbon long enough to tie around a wrist, leaving 3 to 4 inches to hang down at each end.
2. Fold the ribbon in half.
3. Make a slit in the center to fit flower stem.
4. Cut the stem of the flower down to about 2½ inches.
5. Wrap the stem with floral tape.
6. Slide stem into ribbon slit.
7. Place the corsage in a mason jar.
8. Attach a packing tag to the jar.
9. Write the name of the guest on the jar, using a Sharpie.

Hints and Clues

Flower blossoms that look good on their own include cattleya, dendrobium, and cymbidium orchids.

Wrapping the stem with floral tape will protect it and keep it from slipping out of the slit after it's been inserted.

We also filled mason jars with hard-boiled eggs!

Stick in the Moss

You Need

SUPPLIES
Floral oasis

Terra-cotta pots, in a variety
of shapes and sizes

Plastic to line pots

Fresh flowers (freesia, tulips,
nasturtiums)

Floral tape

Moss

Floral pins

1½-inch-wide organdy ribbon

TOOLS
Floral snips

Get Started

1. Soak the oasis in water until it's completely saturated.

2. Line each pot with plastic.

3. Fill each pot with oasis.

4. Strip the flower stems of leaves.

5. Disperse color and size of flowers to create a pleasing arrangement.

6. Gather the stems together just under the blossoms and cut the stems at the bottom, so that the flowers are all the same length, approximately 12 to 15 inches long.

7. Wrap the stems together with floral tape right underneath the blossoms.

8. Keeping the stems together, insert bouquet firmly into oasis.

9. Cover the oasis by taking small pieces of moss and pressing them firmly around the top of the pot. Secure the moss to the oasis with floral pins if necessary.

10. Trim the moss with clippers to create an even edge around the pot.

11. Cut a piece of ribbon twice the length of the stems.

12. Pull each ribbon tail evenly all the way around the stems and tie a knot approximately 2 inches under the blossoms.

13. Pull the tails around again and tie another knot directly under the first knot.

14. Repeat at least four times, ending by tying the two pieces in a bow under the last knot.

Hints and Clues

Be sure to freshen water every few days.

You may want to dig a hole in the center of the oasis before inserting the bouquet so that the stems do not break.

> *Although strictly speaking this is not a topiary, it's my version. Topiary making is really about cutting bushes and hedges to a strict formation and used to be only for the fancy . . . but why not try it yourself? It's fun!*

Frame Game

You Need

SUPPLIES

11 x 14-inch wooden frames

½ inch grosgrain ribbon

11 x 4-inch watercolor paper

TOOLS

Glass cleaner

Paper towels

Scissors

Hot glue gun

Get Started

1. Remove any matting from the frame.

2. Clean the glass with glass cleaner.

3. Cut 6 strips of ribbon in 14-inch lengths.

4. Attach the ribbon horizontally to the paper with a hot glue gun, beginning 1 inch from the top.

5. Repeat with another ribbon ¼ inch below.

6. Skip 2½ inches and repeat process until matte is full.

7. Insert ribbon-covered paper into a frame, ribbon side up.

8. Insert any cardboard filler necessary for tight closure.

Hints and Clues

Wooden frames can be painted any color. Mix different frame designs on your table. Use striped, checked, or plaid ribbon with your frame.

Dream Weaver

Get Started

1. Cut length of ribbon that will equal the length of the four sides of the napkin plus 10 inches.

2. Thread the craft needle with ribbon.

3. Weave the ribbon through the hemstitching over and under, jumping approximately six hemstitches each time, beginning at the corner.

4. Leave two ribbon tails approximately 5 inches long.

Hints and Clues

The woven pattern looks best when each corner is alike, so you might need to adjust spacing so that poufs are spaced evenly.

A large needle makes lacing simple.

Leave ribbon loose to create little poufs.

When purchasing ribbon, measure the length and width of your linen and buy one and one half times that amount.

Be sure to secure the raw edges of the ribbon to prevent raveling.

Wash on the gentle cycle in cold water and lay flat to dry.

Iron linen when still damp. Be careful not to scorch the ribbon.

You Need

SUPPLIES
1½-inch-wide organdy ribbon
Hemstitched linen napkins

TOOLS
Large craft needle

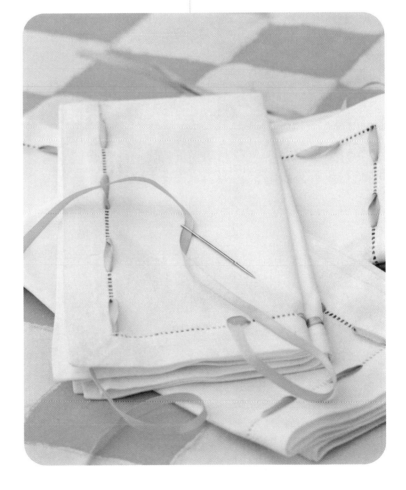

Ham with Garlic and Rosemary

You Need

INGREDIENTS	AMOUNTS
Cooked ham with bone	10 to 12 pounds
Garlic cloves	8, peeled and cut into thin strips
Rosemary sprigs	8
Dark brown sugar	½ cup
Dijon mustard	½ cup
Apple juice or other liquid	2 cups

Get Cookin'

1. Preheat oven to 350°F.
2. Peel the skin from the ham and trim the fat, leaving a ¼-inch layer.
3. Using the tip of a sharp knife, score the fat in a diamond pattern.
4. Insert the sliced garlic and rosemary sprigs into the scores on the ham.
5. Mix the sugar and mustard together and brush on the ham.
6. Place in a shallow roasting pan, add the liquid to the pan, and bake for 1½ hours or until the internal temperature reaches 140° to 150°F.
7. Remove from pan, place ham on a platter, and serve.

Buttermilk Biscuits with Cheddar Cheese

You Need

INGREDIENTS	AMOUNTS
Bisquick	5½ cups
Buttermilk	1⅓ cups
Grated Cheddar cheese	¾ cup (plus ½ cup more for sprinkling tops)
Salt	1 teaspoon
Egg white	1 (for brushing tops)

Get Cookin'

1. Preheat oven to 450°F.

2. Put Bisquick mix in a bowl. With your finger make a well by pushing away the mix at the bottom of the center, like digging in the sand.

3. Pour the buttermilk, cheese, and salt in the center of this well and mix well with your hands. You will now have a soft dough.

4. Place on a slightly floured board and work into a ball.

5. Roll this ball of dough with a rolling pin to a ½-inch thickness.

6. Using a 2½-inch cookie cutter, cut out circles and place on the ungreased cookie sheet.

7. You will now have extra dough (don't throw out!). Roll the extra dough and repeat steps 5 and 6.

8. Take the cut-out biscuits and arrange on a cookie sheet, leaving 1 inch between the cookies.

9. Lightly brush the tops with egg white and sprinkle with the cheese (don't let any fall on the cookie sheet or it will burn during baking).

10. Bake for 8 to 10 minutes, rotating once halfway into baking time for even color.

11. Transfer to a cooling rack.

Fresh Peas with Cream

You Need

INGREDIENTS	AMOUNTS
Fresh or frozen peas	6 cups, cooked
Heavy cream	½ cup
Unsalted butter	3 tablespoons
White onion	4 thin slices
Salt and pepper to taste	

Get Cookin'

1. Cook peas and set aside.
2. Bring the cream to a boil in a saucepan. Turn down heat and let simmer until reduced slightly and thickened.
3. Melt the butter in a small skillet and sauté the onion until translucent.
4. Add the onion and peas to the cream.
5. Heat the peas, season with salt and pepper, and serve immediately.

If you're using fresh peas, it's a good idea to store them in their pods. Don't shell them until right before you are ready to use them.

Mrs. Brown's Scalloped Potatoes

You Need

INGREDIENTS	AMOUNTS
Baking potatoes	1½ per guest (or 18 for 12 people)
Butter	2 tablespoons per layer
Flour	2 tablespoons per layer
Salt and pepper to taste	
Paprika to taste	
Milk or half-and-half to taste (see recipe)	
Bread crumbs	Enough to sprinkle over top

Get Cookin'

1. Preheat oven to 350°F.
2. Peel potatoes and slice into about ¼-inch chip-size slices.
3. Grease a baking dish of appropriate size with butter.
4. Cover the bottom of the dish with a layer of potatoes.
5. Add dollops of butter over the potatoes.
6. Spread flour over the layer.
7. Season with salt, pepper, and paprika.
8. Repeat the layering process until layers reach 1 inch from the top of the dish.
9. Add milk or half-and-half until it just peeks through the top layer of potatoes.
10. Cover top with butter, flour, and bread crumbs.
11. Bake for 1 hour or until the potatoes are tender when tested with a fork.

Almond Apricot Tart

You Need

INGREDIENTS	AMOUNTS
Flour	2 cups
Granulated sugar	½ cup
Salt	½ teaspoon
Unsalted butter	1 cup (2 sticks), at room temperature
FILLING	
Canned apricot halves	4 15¼-ounce cans
Sliced almonds	2 cups
Unsalted butter, melted	8 tablespoons
Granulated sugar	4 tablespoons
Honey	4 tablespoons
Eggs	2, large
Egg white	2, large
Light brown sugar	2 tablespoons

Get Cookin'

1. Preheat oven to 350°F.

CRUST

2. In a food processor, combine the flour, sugar, and salt.

3. Add the butter and pulse until dough resembles cookie dough.

4. Divide dough evenly to create crusts in two 9-inch tart pans. Using fingers, press dough into the pan firmly, building up a ¼-inch-thick rim and finishing with the bottom of the tart.

5. Bake crusts for 10 minutes. Set aside to cool while you make filling.

FILLING

6. Drain apricot halves on paper toweling. Reserve the syrup from 2 cans.

7. Put almonds in a food processor and grind until smooth.

8. Add butter, sugar, and honey and process until blended.

9. Add eggs and egg whites and process until well combined.

10. Divide between the 2 tart pans.

11. Place apricot halves, cut side up, in circular patterns onto the filling, placing one apricot half, cut side down, in the center.

12. Bake for 1 hour or until top is browned and tester comes out clean.

13. Put the reserved apricot syrup in a small pan.

14. Add the brown sugar and bring to a boil.

15. Reduce till syrup thickens and sugar melts.

16. When tart is cool, use a pastry brush to glaze the tart with the syrup and serve the rest of the syrup with the tart.

Did you know that once you open canned food, you should store it in another container if you are not using it all? Once the top is opened and air gets in, the metal on the inside reacts and can no longer keep your food fresh!

6

Simplicity and Salad

A DINNER ON THE ROCKS

PROJECTS

A Darlin' Garland CHAIRS

Bag It! CENTERPIECE

Pebble Place PLACE CARDS

Boxing in Your Table TRIM

Wavy Edge and Swervy Legs TRIM

Rock Garden TABLE

Rocky Road Candles LIGHTING

Rings of Stars NAPKIN RINGS

MENU

Snapper en Papillote

Tabbouleh Katie's Way

Fennel and Orange Salad

Spicy Carrot Salad

Rhubarb-Ginger Pie

if you know me, you know that i love to use bright colors

and patterns. So where did this table come from? It definitely looks different from any of the other tables in this book—I'll bet it looks different from any table you've ever seen—but I think it looks pretty cool!

It all started in the back of a pickup truck. (Don't jump to any conclusions.) It was one of those days . . . my house was a wreck. Why? Well, let's just say it was my first house and I thought things worked a lot faster than they do. I thought it was actually going to be finished on the date I had picked. Amazingly enough, though, on this day everybody who was supposed to be working on my house actually showed up. Painters, plumbers, carpenters—you name it, they were all there. People I had never seen before showed up. And what a mess they made!

I had finally made plans to have lunch with a friend, assuming that once again nobody would show up. Well . . . once they did I wasn't about to leave my house!

We had planned to go out and eat salads only . . . summer was well on its way. When I knew I couldn't go out to lunch, I climbed over to my refrigerator and grabbed everything green I could find, got a little creative, and ran for the door as the drilling really came on full blast.

My friend met me, and, salads in hand, we tromped to the backyard. But the grass was being cut. (Yes, they showed up too!) We were desperate for our lunch, so we just hopped into the back of one of the builder's trucks. The bottom was filled with landscaping rocks, and there was a pile of slate squares in one corner. We sat along the sides of the truck and I pulled out some of the slate squares as makeshift place mats.

As we ate and chatted, I looked down and saw my next tabletop. This was inspiration if I'd ever seen it! The truck was parked under a low-hanging tree and the green from the leaves created a garland in my mind, which, combined with the slate and paper plates, was more than the beginning of this table. Not only did the rocks and slate look pretty great, the salad was made for this table.

When we finished eating, we took some rocks and slate for my later use. (My builder was not so happy when he arrived short on materials for his next job. . . .)

I put most of this table together that night. We've since added a few things here and there and it looks great. If it's simple and it works, I say go with it!

A Darlin' Garland

You Need

SUPPLIES

Pads of inexpensive white
drawing paper

Fishing line

Tacks or nails

TOOLS

Upholstery needles

Hammer

Get Started

1. Crumple paper into firm ball shapes, but not too tight.

2. Thread your upholstery needle with fishing line and string the balls of paper by piercing the balls through the center, continuously forming a garland.

3. Continue stringing balls to the desired length.

4. Tie the fishing line off with a double or triple knot, leaving a good bit of excess.

5. Place small nails or tacks into the right and left corners of the chair backs and hang the garland, using the excess fishing line to attach your garland to the nails. Tie off and trim any excess fishing line.

Hints and Clues

If you don't have fishing line, you may be tempted to use thread—but don't! It will not be strong enough to hold the weight of the balls.

Bag It!

Get Started

1. Roll the top of your paper bag down approximately 2 to 4 inches.

2. Repeat this process with another bag, but be sure to adjust the lip of this bag so that, when finished, you have a doubled bag that gives you a layered look.

3. Remove your plant of choice from its pot and break up the root ball.

4. Fit root and some loose dirt into the layered sacks.

Hints and Clues

This should not be used as a permanent planter, as the paper will disintegrate if mixed with water. After your party you should repot your plants so they are healthy and happy for your next soirée.

We used cyclamen to plant in the bag, but you can use any flowering plant.

> *Did you know that herbalists believe that cyclamen is a "self-esteem builder"? It can help people develop self-confidence.*

You Need

SUPPLIES

White paper lunch bags

White blooming plants
4 to 6 inches

Pebble Place

You Need

SUPPLIES

Large, flat river rocks

TOOLS

Silver paint pens

Get Started

Using a fine-tipped silver paint pen, write the names of each guest on the smoothest surface of your rock and allow to dry.

Hints and Clues

Paint pens need at least 5 minutes drying time, so handle accordingly!

I don't always use place cards, but I wouldn't ever give a party without having some notion of where I wanted people to be seated at the table.

Boxing in Your Table

Get Started

CREATING THE TABLETOP

1. Have a piece of plywood cut to fit over your table.

2. Center the plywood on top of your tabletop (you may want to put a protective layer between the plywood and the tabletop).

CREATING THE GARLAND

3. Hammer one nail into each end of a long board, leaving at least one inch of the nail exposed.

4. Wrap the wire around one nail and extend and tie off at the other nail.

5. Cut the boxwood bunches into 4- to 6-inch lengths. Be sure to leave a bushy green stem at the head of each bunch.

6. Attach the boxwood by placing the first bunch on the wire and wrapping a second wire around the exposed stem, adding additional bunches as the boxwood covering the length of wire. Continue this process until the boxwood has run the length of the wire. The bunches should overlap a bit so that no stems or wires are showing.

TRIMMING THE TABLE

7. Remove the garland and apply it to your tabletop by attaching it to the plywood tabletop with a staple gun. Continue the above step until you have covered the entire perimeter of your tabletop.

Hints and Clues

Remember to keep garland approximately 2 to 3 inches in diameter.

Be sure to hide the staples with your excess greenery.

To help your garland last longer, mist it at least once a day.

You Need

SUPPLIES

Table plywood

2-inch nails with a head

Long board

Medium-gauge wire spool

5 to 6 bunches of boxwood (or other hardy greens), enough to form a garland that will frame your table

TOOLS

Hammer

Staple gun

Wavy Edge and Swervy Legs

Get Started

TABLE EDGE

1. Unroll the corrugated paper onto a flat surface with the ridge side down.
2. Approximately 6 inches from the top (or flat edge), draw a wavelike pattern in pencil that runs the length of your table.
3. Cut along the pencil outline with your scissors.
4. Attach to the edge of the plywood with upholstery tacks.
5. Continue this pattern with the corrugated paper until there is enough cut for the perimeter of your tabletop.

TABLE LEGS

1. Measure the height and width of the table legs.
2. Cut a piece of corrugated paper that will wrap around the table leg.

Hints and Clues

The natural curve of the paper will hold it in place, but occasionally you'll have to tack it down (sometimes a piece of double-stick tape will do the trick, too). You can also hold the corrugated paper in place by tying it tightly around the leg of the table with coordinating paper ribbon.

Make sure to do this project before you attach your boxwood garland, since one of the advantages of your garland will be to cover the upholstery tacks and drape over the paper edges, creating a wonderful finished edge to your tabletop.

You Need

SUPPLIES

2 to 3 rolls of corrugated paper

Upholstery tacks

TOOLS

Pencil

Scissors

Hammer

> *Corrugating is the process of shaping anything into folds or parallel and alternating ridges and grooves.*

Rock Garden

Every summer my sisters and I were signed up—by my mom—for a nature study course. Each morning we would go on long walks to contemplate nature. I could barely stay on the trail; my sister Lynn, however, would fill all of her pockets with different rocks and fossils. When she got her treasures home, she would line cardboard boxes with construction paper, glue her stones all in a row and begin documenting with names and dates. For years, the shelves in her closets had more rocks than sweaters.

You Need

SUPPLIES

Plywood tabletop

Canvas drop cloth

Rectangular or square pieces
   of slate

Medium white marble land-
   scaping rocks

Small white marble landscaping
   rocks

Black Japanese river rocks

TOOLS

Staple gun

Gardening gloves

Get Started

TABLE COVER

1. Cover a piece of plywood with a canvas drop cloth, using a staple gun to attach it to the underside of the plywood.

PLACE MATS

2. Center the pieces of slate in front of each chair as place mats. (Leave a few inches between the place mats; this gap will be filled in later.)

TABLECLOTH

3. Cover the entire tabletop with the medium white landscaping rocks, leaving a border around the edge of the table to fill in with the small white landscaping rocks.

4. Fill in all holes and borders with small white marble landscaping rocks.

RUNNER

5. Make a rectangle down the center of your table with the black Japanese river rocks.

Hints and Clues

Use gardening gloves to protect your hands from the pointy edges of the rocks.

Make sure to move the rocks around the tabletop (à la a jigsaw puzzle) to create as even a surface as possible.

You may want to soak or rinse your rocks before using them.

Rocky Road Candles

You Need

SUPPLIES

1 to 2 pounds paraffin wax in desired color

String

Small, light fishing tackle weights

TOOLS

Double boiler or two-layered saucepans

Scissors

2-inch dowel

1- to 2-feet-deep bucket for dipping

The first time I ever melted paraffin (wax) I was doing a batiking project for my seventh-grade art class. As the wax was heating, the television set distracted me. The next thing I knew, my house was full of firemen. The moral: Don't leave your wax unattended.

Get Started

1. Bring the water in the double boiler to a boil.

2. Melt wax over low heat, but warm enough to keep the wax in liquid form.

3. Cut a piece of string that measures 1 inch longer than the depth of the bucket.

4. Tie the tackle weight to one end of the string.

5. Dip the string into the melted wax to coat it, leaving 1 inch clean of the wax at the top.

6. Tie the coated strings at the top, 2 to 4, depending on the size of your container, to the dowel.

7. Fill the bucket with VERY hot water.

8. Pour the melted wax onto the surface of the hot water and begin to dip the coated strings into the wax, allowing a brief moment between dipping for drying.

9. Hang the candlesticks in a cool place to dry.

10. Cut the string to create a wick at the top of the taper.

Hints and Clues

Keep in mind that these candles should have a very Stone Age/free-form quality to them and will not be smooth.

Something to watch for: Once the water cools, you may have to collect the wax from the surface of your bucket and remelt it and repeat the process till you have the desired thickness to the taper.

We created our double boiler by using the bottom of a double boiler set and substituting the top with a beat-up old pot for wax.

For this particular table we felt the green wax looked best, but there are many colors to choose from, so have fun!

Rings of Stars

Get Started

1. Fold a piece of 5-inch-square white craft paper into an accordion fan.
(The fold should repeat every ¾ inch.)

2. Fold the accordion in half.

3. Starting at the beginning of the fold, cut across in a diagonal.

4. Open and spread the "petals" into a half moon, then lightly glue the space
between the petals.

5. Trim ends into a point. (You now have one side of the napkin ring.)

6. Repeat this process a second time to complete the other half of the napkin ring.

7. Bind together by looping a wire through the crease in the two outer folds.

8. Attach to the plastic tape roll with wire.

9. Use your pliers to tightly twist together and cut off any excess wire.

10. Glue together all loose pieces to form a circular flower shape.

11. Dab glue on to the back where the wire has been joined together and press
on to the white ring.

Hints and Clues

This is the design we have chosen, but any fun or fanciful origami pattern will do.
The rings from first aid tape work great!

The Japanese word origami *means "folding paper":*
ori *means "to fold" and* gami *means "paper."*

You Need

SUPPLIES

Square pieces of
light card stock

Plastic rings from a tape roll
(approximately) 2½ inches
in diameter

TOOLS

Scissors

Wire cutters

Wire

Needle nose pliers

Glue gun and glue sticks

Snapper en Papillote

You Need

INGREDIENTS	AMOUNTS
Parchment paper	1 large sheet
Leeks	¼ cup, white part cut into julienne strips and green leaves reserved
Snapper	2 fillets, 1 pound (skinned)
Red peppers	¼ cup, thinly julienned
Lemon	6 thin slices
Capers	2 tablespoons
Thyme	6 sprigs
White wine	2 tablespoons
Rosemary	4 stalks, 1 foot each
Olive oil	Enough to brush on top
Salt and pepper to taste	

Get Cookin'

For this recipe, you will be cooking, or rather steaming, the snapper fillets in a paper envelope using a method called "en papillote" or "in paper." The fish will rest on a bed of leek greens and will be garnished with lemon, thyme, red peppers, leeks, and capers.

1. Preheat oven to 400°F.
2. Have 1 sheet of parchment paper 16⅜ x 24⅜ inches ready. The size of parchment paper can vary slightly depending on fillet size.
3. Place 2 leek leaves next to each other in the center of the parchment paper, making a bed for the snapper.
4. Season each snapper fillet on both sides with salt and pepper and then lay the snapper on the leek greens.
5. Top the fish with the julienned leeks, red peppers, lemon, capers, and the thyme sprigs.
6. Pour the wine over the fish.
7. To wrap the fish, fold the 2 long ends together and roll the top closed.

8. With a long stalk of rosemary, secure the folds by wrapping them on both ends and tieing.

9. Use a brush to coat the top of the parchment with a thin layer of olive oil. This will help the paper brown during the cooking process.

10. Place the 2 packages on a sheet pan and bake the fish for 15 minutes. Remove from oven and tear open the package from the center. Leave the fish in the papillote and serve, or remove from the paper and serve, using the lemon slices as garnish.

Hints and Clues

Parchment paper is resistant to both grease and moisture, so your pan will stay clean. It can be found in most specialty food shops and many grocery stores have it. Just ask for it by name!

After cooking, the paper can be cut open at the table for dramatic effect, but be careful of the hot steam!

Papillote is the French word for the paper used to decorate the tips of crown roast (you know . . . those white tips that look like crowns!). "En papillote" refers to food wrapped in a special kind of greased parchment paper. As the food cooks in the paper, the heat and steam released create a puff in the top of the paper and the food cooks within the paper in its own juices.

Tabbouleh Katie's Way

You Need

INGREDIENTS	AMOUNTS
Red wine vinegar	¼ cup
Lemon juice	2 tablespoons
Olive oil	⅓ cup plus 2 tablespoons
Water	2 cups
Salt	¼ teaspoon
Couscous	10 ounces
Fresh mint	¼ cup, roughly chopped
Red onion	1, thinly sliced
Cucumber	3 large, peeled and sliced in ¼-inch-thick circles
Roma tomatoes	6, sliced in ¼-inch-thick circles
Garlic clove	1, minced
Salt and pepper to taste	

Get Cookin'

1. To make the dressing, whisk together the vinegar, lemon juice, and ⅓ cup olive oil. Set aside.
2. Bring water, 2 tablespoons olive oil, and salt to a boil in shallow pot.
3. Add couscous, stir, and cover.
4. Remove from heat and let stand for 5 minutes.
5. Place in a bowl and let cool.
6. Add the remaining ingredients and then toss in the dressing and salt and pepper to taste.

Hints and Clues

We chopped the mint in larger pieces and sliced the vegetables in rounds for a more rustic twist on the Mediterranean dish.

The vegetables and couscous can be prepared a day ahead, but do not salt or add dressing to the salad until you are ready to serve, because the salt will soften the cucumbers if they are left to marinate overnight.

Follow the directions for making couscous on the box you buy. Recipes may vary with the brand.

Fennel and Orange Salad

You Need

INGREDIENTS	AMOUNTS
Soy sauce	2 tablespoons
Balsamic vinegar	3 tablespoons
Fresh ginger	1 tablespoon, peeled and minced
Lemon juice	2 tablespoons
Orange juice	1 tablespoon
Water	1 tablespoon
Olive oil	⅓ cup
Green leaf lettuce	2 heads, washed and torn into pieces for a salad
Fennel	2 bulbs, stalks removed, sliced very thin across the root on a mandoline
Oranges	3, peeled and sliced into thin rounds

Get Cookin'

DRESSING

1. To make the dressing, briskly whisk together the soy sauce, vinegar, ginger, lemon juice, orange juice, water, and olive oil. Set aside.

SALAD

2. Toss the greens and fennel together and spread them out on a platter.
3. Make a row of oranges across the top of the salad.

Hints and Clues

To clean the fennel, cut the bulbs in half and run them under cold water. The dirt will run out of the bulb.

Spicy Carrot Salad

You Need

INGREDIENTS	AMOUNTS
Carrots	1 pound, peeled and coarsely chopped or shredded
Paprika	½ teaspoon
Turmeric	½ teaspoon
Cinnamon	½ teaspoon
Lemon juice	3 tablespoons
Olive oil	3 tablespoons
Parsley	¼ cup, coarsely chopped
Salt and pepper to taste	

Get Cookin'

1. Place the grated carrots in a bowl.
2. Add the paprika, turmeric, cinnamon, lemon juice, olive oil, parsley, and salt and pepper. Toss to combine and let stand at room temperature for at least 1 hour to marinate. Toss again and serve.

Hints and Clues

Use a food processor to shred the carrots into a cornmeal consistency.

Rhubarb-Ginger Pie

You Need

INGREDIENTS	AMOUNTS
Frozen rhubarb	1 bag (as sold in supermarket)
Frozen pie dough	4 sheets
Flour	2 tablespoons
Sugar	1 cup, plus more for sprinkling
Vanilla extract	2 teaspoons
Freshly grated ginger	1 tablespoon
Finely grated orange zest	1 tablespoon
Egg	1 large, lightly beaten (for egg wash)
Heavy cream	1 tablespoon (for egg wash)

Get Cookin'

1. Preheat oven to 400°F.

2. Defrost the rhubarb in a large colander placed inside a bowl at room temperature for 1 hour.

3. Unwrap 2 pie crust dough packages and roll out together, one on top of the other, on a lightly floured surface. (The 2 layers will make a nice, thick crusty wrap for the pie.)

4. Place on a parchment-lined baking sheet and refrigerate until ready to use.

5. Gently squeeze the rhubarb to remove excess liquid.

6. In a large bowl, mix the defrosted and drained rhubarb with the flour, sugar, vanilla extract, grated ginger, and orange zest.

7. Let stand 10 to 15 minutes.

8. Fill the dough with the rhubarb mixture, leaving a 2-inch border all around the outside. When rhubarb filling is in place, gently pull the dough up over the filling until it is completely encircled, making folds around the circumference.

9. In a small bowl, whisk together the egg and cream for the egg wash.

10. Using a pastry brush, gently brush the dough with the egg wash and sprinkle it generously with sugar.

11. Place pie in oven in a pie dish and bake until the dough is golden brown and the filling is hot and bubbling, 35 to 45 minutes.

7

Santa Fe Fantasy

A DINNER FOR SIX

PROJECTS

Desert Blooms CENTERPIECE

Sage Smudge Sticks FAVORS

Sand De-Lites LIGHTING

Slate Stilts TABLE

Stumped CHAIRS

Sandy Sunsets TABLETOP

MENU

BBQ Pork Marinated in
Tequila and Coriander

Black Bean Cakes

Roasted Corn Salsa

Oven-roasted Tortilla Chips

Caramel Flan

Santa Fe Fantasy A DINNER FOR SIX

everybody feels the need to get away from it all

sometimes. In fact . . . in my experience, most people I know fantasize about fleeing from it all on a regular basis. It really doesn't matter if a person likes his or her life, job, or home; it's just that sometimes everybody wants to get AWAY!

Where do people want to go? The answer is a bit different for each person. Everyone has a different idea, but there is some common ground. If you came into my fantasy, and I came into yours, we would each leave with something different.

Well . . . it was one of those times for my friend Marge.

She called me and said, "Katie—I've had it; I'm not going to work today. I'm not going to work tomorrow, and I'm not going next week. I'm coming over in a few hours. Pack a bag. We're going to watch the sunset in Santa Fe; we're going to see turquoise and silver and cacti and whatever, but I want out of here!"

I hung up the phone and thought about it. *I* didn't want to go to New Mexico that afternoon. Although I wouldn't have minded a little escape; I just *had* to show up for work in the morning. I couldn't fly away that day. Yet, I wouldn't mind escaping to my *dining room* . . .

What could I do? I knew I couldn't let Marge down. I looked around my house. Where could we go? Hmm . . . then it clicked; Santa Fe, New Mexico, she wanted . . . Santa Fe she would get! I started out with the turquoise rocks from the bottom of my fishbowl. By the time I was done, Marge's fantasy was right in my dining room! Her cacti and her sand; red hot from the sun, candles and burlap—it was all there!

Maybe you want to escape to the Southwest—or maybe you need to go to Alaska. Wherever it is, be a little creative and you'll find it's no farther than your own home! That way you'll be ready for work the very next day—Marge sure was!

Desert Blooms

You Need

SUPPLIES

Plastic bags

Sand

Burlap

½- to 2-foot-tall branches
(without leaves)

Floral wire

Twine

TOOLS

Garden clippers

Scissors

Get Started

1. Fill a thick plastic bag with sand.

2. Place the bag onto a square of burlap that is large enough to cover the entire bag.

3. Arrange 10 to 12 branches in a bunch.

4. Wrap the bottoms together with floral wire.

5. Drive the bottoms of the branches into the center of the sandbag.

6. Loosely gather the burlap up around the bag and tie the neck with twine, creating a bag shape.

7. Wrap a 2- to 3-foot length of twine all around the burlap sack, pulling the twine over and under, crisscrossing and pretty much just randomly creating a haphazard design on the burlap bag.

8. Tie the neck tightly by wrapping twine around and around and tying it off in a knot.

9. Place two or three bundles down the center of the table.

Hints and Clues

Look for interesting-shaped branches.

Make sure to tie the neck of the sack tightly.

The first year GOAT was open, I knew we had to get a holiday tree come December. I told my partner, Sara. She said, "Let me take care of it, Katie, I make trees!" Huh . . . ? Well, she came into work the next day with an 8-foot-tall Christmas tree made from branches— no needles! She had glued the whole thing together and put it in a burlap bag. It was amazing!

Sage Smudge Sticks

You Need

SUPPLIES
Fresh or dried sage

Twine

TOOLS
Scissors

Clippers

Get Started

1. Gather a bundle of 6 to 8 sage leaves that are about 7 to 10 inches long. Create a cigar-shape roll with all the sage leaves facing the same way.

2. Wrap twine down the length of the leaf bundle in 3 to 5 different areas, about 1 inch apart, each tied with a knot.

Hints and Clues

You can use the leaves on or off the stems.

If you choose to wrap fresh leaves, allow time for them to dry in their bundle as they must be dry to burn.

Did you know that smudge sticks are a part of many Native American traditions and are still used in rituals?

Sand De-Lites

You Need

SUPPLIES
25-pound bag of play sand

6 ounces yellow food coloring

6 various-sized pillar candles

Spray adhesive

TOOLS
Tin tub

Protective rubber gloves

Get Started

DYEING THE SAND
1. Put sand in the tub.

2. Put on gloves.

3. Add several drops of food coloring to the sand.

4. Mix well with your hands.

COVERING THE CANDLE
1. Pick up a candle, holding it by the wick.

2. Spray the candle with adhesive, rotating it in order to cover all sides and the top.

3. Roll the candle in the dyed sand.

4. Place sand-covered candles down the center of the table.

Hints and Clues
Make sure not to coat the sand too thickly near the wick because it will make it harder to light.

Slate Stilts

....

Get Started

BUILDING THE LEGS

1. Mix the cement in a bucket, following directions on the bag.

2. Stack the fieldstone pieces one on top of the other, putting a layer of cement between each.

3. Make legs, each the same height—whatever height you wish your table to be.

PLACING THE TABLETOP

1. Spread a layer of cement over the top of all four legs.

2. Lay the piece of plywood across the legs.

3. If the tabletop does not lay flat, even it out by adding cement to the top of the legs.

4. Allow the cement to dry.

Hints and Clues

The stone doesn't need to be exactly square.

Make sure that you use your flattest and largest pieces of slate on the top and bottom of the legs.

> *While cut-to-order slate can be expensive, various-sized chunks are available at many hardware/home stores or at masonry supply stores.*

You Need

SUPPLIES

Cement
   (approximately ½ of a bucket)
Fieldstone pieces
   1–1½ feet each
Plywood suitable for tabletop

TOOLS

Bucket
Protective rubber gloves
Spatula

Stumped

You Need

SUPPLIES

Collection of sitting stools

Brown spray paint

Burlap

Wood stain

2-inch-wide wood molding

TOOLS

Sandpaper

Scissors

Cloth rag

Handsaw

Nails

Hammer

If you don't feel like putting a hem in something, fringe the ends . . . it works.

Get Started

1. Clean and lightly sand stools.

2. Spray-paint the stools the same color as the wood stain of the trim.

3. Cut a square piece of burlap to fit over the stool top, leaving 6 to 8 inches of skirting on all sides.

4. Stain the molding by dipping the cloth rag into the wood stain and rubbing the stain onto the molding. Let molding dry.

5. Saw the molding to match the length of the four sides of the stool. Be sure to make two sides longer to create a frame of finished edges.

6. Nail the molding through the burlap into the edge of the stool.

7. Touch up any raw molding with the stain.

8. Fringe the burlap skirting by continually removing the horizontal weave in the burlap until desired fringe length is achieved.

9. Trim the length with scissors.

Sandy Sunsets

Get Started

PREPARING THE TABLETOP

1. Put sand in a tin tub.

2. Put on protective rubber gloves.

3. Add several drops of food coloring to the sand.

4. Mix well with your hands.

5. Mix ½ cup of water to ½ cup of glue.

6. Paint a quarter section of the plywood with the glue mixture (paint in quarters so that the glue mixture does not dry too quickly).

7. Pour the sand over the glue and lightly press it.

8. Repeat this process until the table is covered with sand.

9. Allow to dry.

FRINGING THE TABLE (in the same pattern as the stool)

1. Cut a strip of burlap about 8 inches wide to go all the way around the table.

2. Staple the burlap into the edge of the plywood.

3. Stain the molding by dipping the cloth into the wood stain and rubbing it onto the wood molding. Let molding dry.

4. Cut the molding with a handsaw to frame the border of the tabletop.

5. Nail the molding to the tabletop, using 1-inch brads.

6. Fringe the burlap skirting by gently pulling out the horizontal weave of the burlap, creating a fringe of about 4 inches, leaving 3 to 4 inches of solid skirting.

CREATING THE DESIGN ON THE TABLETOP

1. Cut off about 1 inch of the corner of a thick plastic bag creating a pastry bag. You will be pouring the aquarium rocks through the hole, which creates a bit more control.

2. Fill the bag with aquarium rocks and pour them down the middle of the table in a 2-inch-wide curved pattern that runs the length of the table.

3. Return to the beginning of the line and create curled arms on both sides of the pattern about 10 to 12 inches apart.

Hints and Clues

You may want to make one practice pour of the rocks before pouring on the actual table.

You Need

SUPPLIES

50 pounds sand

10 ounces red food coloring

White glue

Plywood tabletop

Burlap

Wood stain

2-inch-wide wood molding

1-inch wire brads

Thick plastic bag

Aquarium rocks

TOOLS

Tin tub

Protective rubber gloves

Paintbrush

Scissors

Staple gun

Cloth rag

Handsaw

Hammer

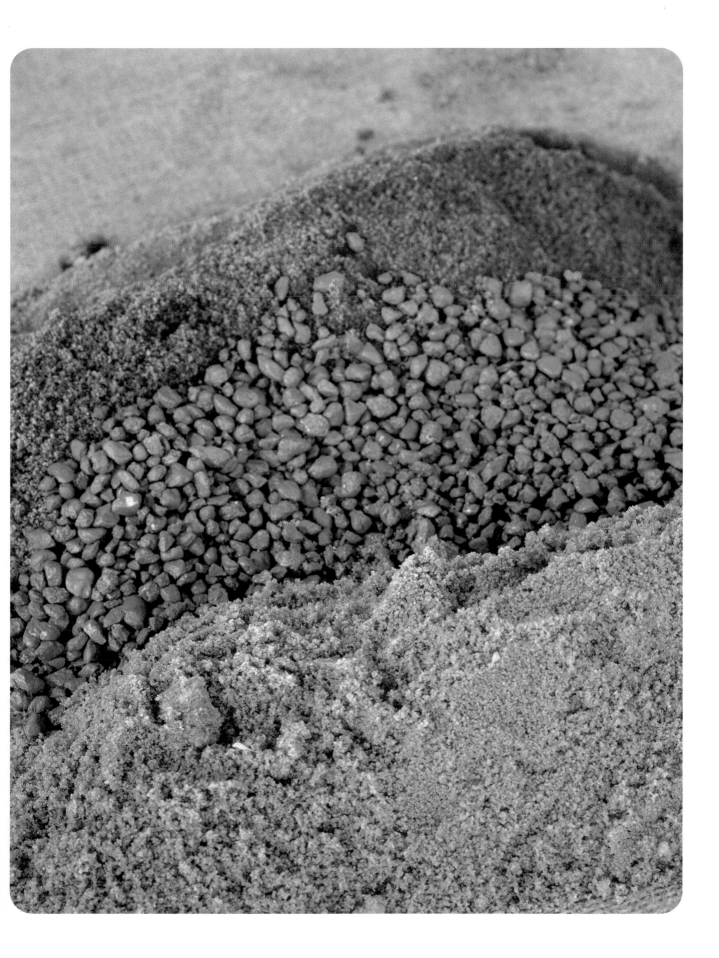

BBQ Pork Marinated in Tequila and Coriander

You Need

INGREDIENTS	AMOUNTS
Tequila	4 tablespoons
Olive oil	4 tablespoons
Garlic	6 cloves, chopped
Jalapeños	2, chopped (yields 2 tablespoons)
Lime juice	2 limes, 3 tablespoons
Coriander seeds	1 teaspoon, crushed
Canned chopped tomatoes or fresh plum tomatoes	1 can or 3 fresh, chopped, plus 1 cup, diced, for garnish
Pork loin	3 pounds, bone removed
Salt	½ tablespoon
Pepper	1 teaspoon
Molasses	2 tablespoons
Brown sugar	3 tablespoons

Get Cookin'

1. Preheat oven to 400°F.

2. Make marinade by combining the tequila, 2 tablespoons of olive oil, garlic, jalapeños, lime juice, coriander seeds, and tomatoes. Pour marinate into a shallow baking dish.

3. Add pork to the marinade and let marinate for at least 2 hours or up to 12 hours. Turn the pork occasionally to ensure that all sides are marinated.

4. Remove the pork from the baking dish, reserving the marinade, and pat the loin dry. Heat remaining 2 tablespoons of olive oil in a pan until just smoking.

5. Salt and pepper the pork and place in the hot pan, fat side down first.

6. Sear the loin for about 3 minutes per side, until a nice crust forms.

7. Place the pork in a Pyrex dish and place in the oven.

8. In the pan used for the searing, add the reserved marinade and turn the heat to high. Bring the marinade to a boil and add the molasses and brown sugar. Cook for 2 minutes, then remove from heat.

9. Place the glaze into a bowl and, using a brush, baste the pork loin.

10. Continue to baste every 15 minutes until the pork is done.

11. When the internal temperature of the pork reaches 145°F on a meat thermometer, remove the pork from the oven and allow to stand at least 5 minutes before serving.

12. Remove the strings (if any) and slice loin in ¼-inch slices.

13. Garnish with chopped plum tomatoes.

Hints and Clues

You can omit the alcohol from the marinade.

Canned jalapeños can be substituted for fresh.

You can use bottled lime juice instead of fresh, if needed.

Black Bean Cakes

You Need

INGREDIENTS	AMOUNTS
Black beans (canned)	4 cups, run under water and well drained
Scallions	½ cup, thinly sliced
Roasted red peppers	½ cup, julienned
Flour	6 tablespoons, plus more for dusting
Tabasco sauce	2 teaspoons
Salt	2 teaspoons
Pepper	1 teaspoon
Canola oil	6 tablespoons
Sour cream	1 cup
Chives	2 tablespoons, sliced in 1-inch pieces

Get Cookin'

1. In a bowl or food processor, lightly mash the beans, keeping some large pieces intact but creating some paste.
2. Mix the beans together with the scallions, peppers, flour, Tabasco sauce, salt, and pepper.
3. Form black bean patties in your hand about half the size of a hamburger.
4. Dust both sides of the patties with flour.
5. Heat the oil in a pan over medium heat for about 3 minutes, until the oil is very hot.
6. Fry the cakes for about 5 minutes on each side, until the outside is crispy and lightly fried.
7. Top with sour cream that has been mixed with chives.

Hints and Clues

Make sure the oil is hot before frying the cakes or the outside will not be crispy.

Do not crowd the pan with the cakes when frying. If you need to make them in batches, place the fried cakes on a sheet pan and when all have been fried, place the sheet pan in the oven at 350°F for 5 minutes to warm them through.

Did you know that black beans are also called turtle beans?

Roasted Corn Salsa

You Need

INGREDIENTS	AMOUNTS
Corn	6 ears (6 cups), kernels removed and placed on foil-lined baking sheet
Olive oil	3 tablespoons, plus 1 teaspoon
Red onion	1 small, diced
Cilantro	¼ cup, finely chopped
Jalapeño	2 teaspoons, minced
Lime juice	3 tablespoons, fresh
Sugar	2 teaspoons
Salt	2 teaspoons

Get Cookin'

1. Preheat oven to 450°F.
2. Toss the corn in 1 teaspoon of olive oil and place in the oven. Roast the kernels until they start to brown slightly. This should take about 15 minutes.
3. Remove corn from oven and allow to cool.
4. Place the remaining ingredients in a bowl, add the corn, and mix.

Hints and Clues

If fresh corn is unavailable, you can substitute frozen corn that has been thawed.

You can substitute bottled lime juice for fresh.

To accelerate the cooling of the roasted corn, place the corn in the refrigerator to cool.

To remove kernels from a cob, first remove the husks and silk. Cut off the stem bottom to make a flat bottom. Use a chef's knife or a serrated knife to cut the kernels off; start at the top of the cob and cut straight down.

Oven-roasted Tortilla Chips

You Need

INGREDIENTS	AMOUNTS
Canola oil	¼ cup
Fajita-size flour tortillas	1 11.5-ounce package
Salt	1 teaspoon
Paprika	2 teaspoons
Cayenne pepper	1 teaspoon

Get Cookin'

1. Preheat oven to 400°F.

2. Oil a cookie sheet.

3. Brush oil on both sides of each tortilla.

4. Combine salt, paprika, and cayenne pepper and mix together.

5. Sprinkle tortillas with the salt mixture.

6. Cut tortillas into wedges and place on cookie sheet.

7. Place in oven and roast for 8 to 10 minutes, or until chips begin to turn brown and crisp. Repeat until you've used all the tortillas.

Hints and Clues

You can also use corn tortillas for a different texture.

Use more or less cayenne pepper, depending on how spicy you want the chips.

Caramel Flan

You Need

INGREDIENTS	AMOUNTS
CUSTARD	
Milk	1 quart
Eggs	6 large
Egg yolks	5
Sugar	¾ cup
Cinnamon	2 tablespoons
CARAMEL	
Sugar	2 cups
Water	½ cup

Get Cookin'

1. Preheat the oven to 350°F.

MAKE THE CUSTARD

2. Heat the milk until small bubbles appear on the top but do not boil.

3. Beat the eggs, yolks, sugar, and cinnamon together until incorporated.

4. Slowly beat in the warm milk, trying not to create bubbles.

MAKE THE CARAMEL

5. In a heavy 1½-quart saucepan with cover, bring the sugar and water combination to a boil. Let it cook until it returns to a granulated form, continually stirring and watching until it again turns brown and turns to a liquid caramel form. Once golden, continue to stir (so that it doesn't burn) until you have a smooth caramel.

6. Remove the caramel from heat and place the saucepan in an ice water bath to stop it from cooking. Set aside.

CREATING THE FINAL FLAN

7. Pour ¼ inch of caramel in the bottom of foil ramekins. Swirl ramekins around to coat the sides.

8. Fill the ramekins to the top with custard and place them in a Pyrex dish.

9. Pour hot water into the Pyrex dish, filling it so that the water reaches ¾ up the sides of the ramekins. (The dish should be big enough so the ramekins don't touch.)

Flan and crème caramel are the same thing, but one is eaten in Spanish-speaking countries, and one in French-speaking countries. Crème Brûlée is crème caramel with a sugared top that is then melted quickly (either under a broiler or with a blowtorch) until it hardens.

10. Place dish in oven and cook for 25 minutes, or until the custard is set when tested with a skewer.

11. Remove ramekins from the hot bath and refrigerate for 1 hour.

12. When ready to serve, run a knife carefully around the edge of the custard. Invert the crème caramel onto the serving plate and serve.

Hints and Clues

Reserve the extra caramel sauce and when ready to serve, heat the sauce and pour over the dessert to finish. If bubbles form when you temper the milk into the eggs and sugar, use a spoon or ladle to remove them before filling up the ramekins.

Katie's Great Calm by the Sea

8

A TWILIGHT DINNER FOR FOUR

MENU

Steamed Cod with Mango
and Avocado Relish

Gazpacho

Quick Herbed Flat Bread

Sugar Snap Peas Dressed with Tarragon

Strawberry Fool

PROJECTS

Gilligan's Banquet TABLE

Seashells by the Silverware NAPKIN RINGS

Sitting Seaside CHAIRS

Table Tikis LIGHTING

Sandbox CENTERPIECE

Message in a Bottle FAVORS

Freeze-Frond! ICE BUCKET

Frond-tastick PLACE MATS

Weavin' and Steamin' PLATES

after i signed the contract for my house on Long Island

I remember the feeling of needing air—lots of it—immediately! I'd certainly never spent so much money before—and what for—a "house" made up from two barns attached by an old butcher shop. What was I thinking? Surely I didn't just sign on the dotted line for this?

I shook hands etc., etc., with everybody and sent them all away. The previous owners had moved out months before so the house really was mine . . . totally. *Air, Katie . . . air . . .* the more and more I looked around at the barn roof with visible holes, the 4 glass sliding doors serving as windows . . . I knew I needed air and lots of air or I was going to pass out. What had I done?

I hopped in my car and took the quick trip over to the beach. The beach. There it was. This was one of the reasons I wanted to be near the sea, right? It was late October, crisp air but with a hint of summer still left everywhere. And of course no other people but me. Perfect . . . even on that fateful-feeling day, I had to admit it. If nothing else felt like it was . . . the beach was just perfect.

I took deep breaths, sat down, and listened to the waves. And again, I slowly started to feel good about my house . . . yes . . . MY OWN HOUSE . . . that sounded pretty good . . . it wasn't wrong! And the ocean . . . Michigan girl discovers the sea . . . I liked it! Okay . . . I was getting in control.

Things *would* be all right. They would! As I breathed it all in I realized that things HAD to be all right and pretty fast. And you know what? I spent a few hours on the beach and nothing fell apart. I went back to that house and was not afraid. It worked.

Because I grew up on Lake Michigan, I didn't spend a lot of time near the ocean. It was not until I was older that I came to love the ocean as I do now. It has become my own place, whereas the lake is a place I share with my family. The ocean frequently comes to my rescue. Atlantic, Pacific, whatever . . . I know that the sea will always be there to soothe me. I love the shells and the sand, the waves and the dunes. It is a place I can go to escape, but when I am on Long Island I never have to go very far. Sometimes, all I have to do is think about it and I can get through the week knowing I'll be there soon! Occasionally, if I am in the city and know I can't drive right over to the beach, all I have to do is put a conch shell up to my ear, and I know everything will be all right. The sounds of the sea are like a miracle. Try it!

Gilligan's Banquet

You Need

SUPPLIES

2 straw beach mats

Wooden table

Grass skirting

Nails with a broad head

Bamboo poles

1 bamboo roll-up blind

TOOLS

Scissors

Handsaw

Staple gun

Hammer

Hot glue gun

Get Started

TABLETOP

1. Cut the beach mats to fit the tabletop.

2. Staple gun the mats down along the edges of the tabletop.

TABLE SIDE

3. Attach grass skirting to the side edge of the table with the hammer and nails.

TABLE EDGE

4. Cut bamboo poles to fit all 4 sides of table.

5. Glue the bamboo to the top outside edge of table, creating a frame.

TABLE LEGS

6. Cut shade to fit around table legs. As you cut the shade, apply hot glue to the stitches that hold the shade together (this will keep the shade from unraveling).

7. Attach shade around the table legs with hot glue.

Hints and Clues

It might be necessary to trim your grass skirting. We found a strong pair of scissors did the job, but a handsaw will also work.

Bamboo was brought into Europe in the 1820s from Asia and became a popular source of both decoration and furniture. Bamboo is now grown naturally in North America, southern Chile, China, and the Himalayas. Although bamboo grows rapidly, there is a scarcity of it in China, where bamboo forests have been totally cleared to make room for people. This has led to the unfortunate depletion of the bamboo-eating panda bear population, which has dwindled to under 1,000 worldwide.

Seashells by the Silverware

Get Started

1. Choose as many seashells and starfish as guests—your shells should have a bit of meat to them, say 3 inches or so.

2. Using a hot glue gun, attach the shells or starfish to the metal attachment on each hair elastic.

3. Hold shell in place until hot glue hardens.

4. Once glue has cooled, insert napkin.

Hints and Clues

To get the fish smell of the sea out of the shells, soak them for 24 hours in bleach and water.

You Need

SUPPLIES

Seashells

Starfish

Hair elastics

TOOLS

Hot glue gun

Sitting Seaside

You Need

SUPPLIES
Large philodendron leaves
Slat-backed chairs
Raffia
Stick-tac

TOOLS
Scissors

Did you know that philodendron plants are great plants for busy people? Although their optimum conditions are medium sunlight and moist soil, if they don't happen to get their sun or their water, they still persevere!

Get Started

1. Place a philodendron leaf on the back of your chair and tie it in place with a long, thick stream of raffia (it will be easy to do because of the natural openings in the leaf). Finish off with a bold knot and let the raffia stream down the back of the chair.
2. Repeat the above step a couple of more times down the back of the chair.
3. Use a dot of Stick-tac or waterproof floral tape to attach each "petal" of the leaf to the back of the chair; this keeps the leaves from flapping in the wind and tearing.

Hints and Clues
This is a great way to dress up any type of chair.

Table Tikis

Get Started

1. Bamboo poles have natural knots along their shoots. With a handsaw, cut approximately 1 inch above each knot. Each cut will give you a piece of bamboo to use as a candlestick. You will have 5 to 6 pieces per rod. Each piece will vary in size.
2. Begin attaching the scallop shells to the base by covering the bottom rim of the shoot with hot glue.
3. Hold shell in place until glue begins to harden.
4. On each side of the base shell, attach another scallop shell until all 4 sides are covered.
5. Insert tapers into the bamboo shoots, trimming taper bases as necessary.

Hints and Clues

Test different shells on the base before attaching to see which ones will best balance your candlestick.

You Need

SUPPLIES
Bamboo poles
Scallop shells
Taper candles

TOOLS
Handsaw
Hot glue gun

Use a variety of lighting when you are giving a party and place lights at many different levels. I like to use lots of candles at every party I give!

Sandbox

You Need

SUPPLIES
Square ready-made artist's
canvas
Assorted seashells
Sand

TOOLS
Hot glue gun

Get Started

1. Place the canvas on a worktable so it's sitting like a bowl.
2. Apply a generous amount of hot glue to a shell and place around rim, holding in place until glue dries. Continue adding shells until rim is covered.
3. Fill the center with sand.

Hints and Clues

Artist's canvas is easily found at art supply stores. For this project, the deeper the better. In addition to shells, you can also use starfish, sand dollars, etc.

My family uses my favorite dishes and glasses in the summer. My grandmother picked them out in Italy many years ago, and we've used them ever since. They are thick and bright and remind me of summer, sand, and swimming. If I think about them, I know the warm weather will be just around the corner . . .

Message in a Bottle

You Need

SUPPLIES
Paper
Small glass bottles
Pencils
Corks

In sixteenth-century England, messages in bottles were considered possible threats to national security. Any bottles with messages had to be brought to court, still sealed, for the government to open.

In 1949 a bottle was found with a will in it. The will turned out to be that of the heir to much of the Singer sewing machine fortune. Who was the beneficiary? "The person who finds and claims this bottle," of course!

Get Started

1. Roll the paper up small enough to fit through the top of your bottle.
2. Slide the roll into the bottle.
3. Slide in a small pencil.
4. Cork it.

Hints and Clues

Incorporate this idea into the end of your party by making each guest write out a wish and toss it into the ocean; it is sure to end the evening on a magical note!

Plan a follow-up party to be hosted by the person whose message is first received . . . whenever that might be!

This idea can also be used as an invite . . . just include the necessary information on the paper scroll before you close it up in the bottle and leave it in someone's mailbox.

Freeze-Frond!

Get Started

1. Attach the lemon leaves to the plastic container from top to bottom using a dab of hot glue on the back of each leaf. Cover the entire container.

2. Cut the upper chunk of the palm fronds to the approximate height of your bucket.

3. Apply hot glue to the center stem of the palm frond and adhere to the lemon leaves. Do this in 4 places, one on each "side" of the container.

4. Finish off your ice bucket by tying the plain stem of a palm frond around the container.

Hints and Clues

We lined the inside lip of the container with lemon leaves for a more finished look.

The palm stem not only adds a finishing touch but it also helps keep the palm fronds in place.

You Need

SUPPLIES

Fresh lemon leaves

Plastic container or a bucket

4 fresh palm fronds

TOOLS

Hot glue gun

Floral snips

I once bought an ice bucket at a swap meet for $8.00 to sell at GOAT. I stuck a $16.00 price tag on the old gray thing, figuring maybe I'd get about $12.00 for it. That very day a man came in and gave me $16.00 with no questions asked. He came back the next day with a gorgeous, shiny sterling silver bin. It was my ice bucket, which was actually a fabulous Gorham antique. That very day I decided to learn everything about silver that I could, and I haven't made that mistake again!

Frond-tastick

You Need

SUPPLIES
Fresh palm fronds

Leaf shine

TOOLS
Scissors

Hot glue gun

Get Started

1. Trim individual palms from their stem (the longer lengths are preferable; if the palm leaves are too short, connect them with a dot of hot glue to make longer pieces).
2. On a flat surface, begin weaving the palms, using the traditional over-and-under weaving method. Add a dot of hot glue where necessary. Size place mats to 11 x 14 inches.
3. Spray mats with leaf shine for a healthy glow.

Hints and Clues

The palms do not create a tight place mat. The nature of the leaves will make the place mat somewhat fragile to handle, so be careful.

Palm fronds can dry out rather quickly, so assembling your place mats as close to party time is a good idea.

You can use the stripped palm stem and use it for the Freeze-Frond ice bucket.

Weavin' and Steamin'

You Need

SUPPLIES

Fresh palm fronds

Bamboo steamer

Get Started

1. Weave a single palm leaf in and out of the bottom of your steamer.

2. Weave next palm leaf opposite to the first leaf.

3. Continue the same process until you have covered the first 3 inches of the steamer bottom.

4. Skip 3 inches and repeat the same process.

5. Continue alternating woven and nonwoven areas until the bottom of the steamer is covered.

Hints and Clues

You can still use the steamer to cook your meal; it will not affect or hurt the taste of the food.

Steamed Cod with Mango and Avocado Relish

You Need

INGREDIENTS	AMOUNTS
RELISH	
Mangoes	2, diced
Avocados	2, diced
Cherry tomatoes	½ cup, quartered
Cilantro	2 tablespoons, chopped
Fresh lime juice	1 tablespoon
Honey	1 teaspoon
Red pepper flakes	1 teaspoon
Olive oil	2 tablespoons
Salt	1 teaspoon
Pepper	¼ teaspoon
Cod	4 6-ounce fillets
Salt	1 teaspoon
Pepper	½ teaspoon
Vidalia onions	2, sliced in ½-inch circles
Fresh lemon juice	1 tablespoon

Get Cookin'

1. Mix the mangoes, avocados, tomatoes, cilantro, lime juice, honey, pepper flakes, and olive oil gently in a bowl. Season with salt and pepper and set aside.
2. Season the cod with salt and pepper.
3. Lay the sliced onions in a steamer, lay the cod on the bed of onions, and place the steamer over boiling water. Do not allow the water to touch the fish or it will poach instead of steam.
4. Cover the steamer tightly and cook the fish for about 5 to 6 minutes or until cooked through.
5. To serve, squeeze lemon juice over the fish and top with the mango and avocado relish.

Hints and Clues

If cod is unavailable, you can substitute any other flaky white fish, such as snapper or whitefish. When mixing the relish, do so gently so that it does not come out mushy.

Did you know that Cape Cod is named because the shape is like a cod? Keep in mind that scrod is any piece of cod weighing 2 pounds or under.

Gazpacho

You Need

INGREDIENTS	AMOUNTS
Cucumbers	2 medium, quartered
Red bell peppers	2, seeded and quartered
Yellow pepper	1, seeded and quartered
Red onion	1, quartered
Plum (Roma) tomatoes	6, quartered
Garlic clove	1, minced
Tomato juice	4 cups
Red wine vinegar	¼ cup
Fresh lime juice	1 medium lime
Fresh dill	¼ cup, chopped
Salt and pepper to taste	

Get Cookin'

1. Place the cucumbers, red bell peppers, yellow pepper, and red onion one at a time in a food processor and pulse until chopped but not minced. You can chop the red and yellow peppers together if you wish.
2. Place the chopped vegetables in a large bowl and add the remaining ingredients. Stir and refrigerate for 2 hours or overnight before serving.

Hints and Clues

The favors of the gazpacho will "bloom" the longer it sits.
You can substitute canned chopped tomatoes for the plum tomatoes.
Rolling lemons or limes in the palms of your hands can help to get their juices flowing.

Every dinner party at GOAT started with a big tureen of soup, cold or hot. One reason I love this recipe is because the Kitchen Aid food processor does all the work!

Quick Herbed Flat Bread

You Need

INGREDIENTS	AMOUNTS
Warm water	1 cup
Active dry yeast	1 package (¼ ounce or 7 grams)
Flour	2½ to 3 cups
Salt	½ teaspoon
Olive oil	2 tablespoons
Fresh thyme	2 tablespoons, chopped
Fresh rosemary	2 tablespoons, finely chopped
Fresh sage	1 tablespoon, roughly chopped
Fresh Italian flat-leaf parsley	2 tablespoons, roughly chopped

Get Cookin'

1. Preheat grill to medium-high, or preheat oven to 500°F.

2. Combine the water, yeast and 1½ cups of the flour in a large bowl. Mix well. Add the salt, oil, and the rest of the flour.

3. Mix these ingredients together with your hands or with a wooden spoon until incorporated and the dough holds its shape.

4. Knead the dough on a lightly floured surface for about 5 minutes until the dough feels elastic. If the dough feels sticky, add a little more flour.

5. Lightly oil a large bowl.

6. Place the dough in the bowl and cover with plastic wrap. Allow the dough to rise until it has doubled in size, which should take about an hour.

7. Place the risen dough on a lightly floured surface and divide it into 8 balls of equal size.

8. Fold in the fresh herbs by placing the dough in the palm of your hands, sprinkling it with herbs, folding it, and repeating the process. Push down with palms if bread becomes too tall.

9. Brush the top with olive oil.

10. Cook on a grill, about 7 to 10 minutes per side. You can also bake it in the oven on a preheated pizza pan for 15 to 20 minutes.

Sugar Snap Peas Dressed with Tarragon

You Need

INGREDIENTS	AMOUNTS
Sugar snap peas	1 pound
Water	2 tablespoons
Olive oil	1 tablespoon
Fresh tarragon	1 tablespoon, chopped
Salt	1 tablespoon

Get Cookin'

1. Trim the sugar snap peas by cutting off the top and bottom.
2. Fill a sauté pan with the water, olive oil, tarragon, and salt. Bring to a boil and then add the sugar snap peas.
3. Reduce the heat and simmer until done, approximately 3 minutes.

Hints and Clues

You can substitute frozen sugar snap peas for fresh if they are unavailable.
You can also steam the sugar snap peas with the herbs and seasonings.

Flat bread comes from traditional Scandinavian crisps. In Scandinavia, the thin, crackerlike bread is usually made with rye flour. Some crisps are based on combinations of wheat, barley, or potato flours . Lavash is a very thin oblong or square bread of Armenian origin, served from the pan. It can be trimmed as needed.

Strawberry Fool

You Need

INGREDIENTS	AMOUNTS
Strawberries	6 cups
Orange juice	¼ cup
Granulated sugar	¼ cup
Heavy cream	2 cups
Powdered sugar	1 tablespoon
Vanilla extract	2 teaspoons

Get Cookin'

1. Place the strawberries in a bowl and add the orange juice and granulated sugar.

2. Toss the mixture with your hands and let sit for 15 minutes.

3. Whip the heavy cream in a mixer and sprinkle in the powdered sugar and vanilla extract. Beat until it forms stiff peaks (like marshmallows).

4. Set the mix aside and refrigerate.

5. Take the strawberries that have been sitting out and place 4 cups in a blender, reserving 2 cups.

6. Blend till smooth, transfer to a bowl, and place in the freezer for 10 minutes.

7. Take the cream out of the refrigerator and take the strawberry puree out of the freezer. Combine with a whisk.

8. Place a small amount of the mixture in a serving glass.

9. Arrange some of the reserved strawberries (3 or 4), then cover with more cream. Top off with a whole strawberry if you like. Cover each top with plastic wrap and refrigerate for at least 1 hour.

The Color Guard

A DINNER FOR EIGHT

PROJECTS

Flag 'em Down PLACE MATS

Colored Ponds CENTERPIECE

Paint the Town Red PLATES AND GLASSES

Green Means Go TABLETOP

Ready ... Dip ... Go! FAVORS

Sea Legs TABLE AND CHAIRS

Napkins to Dye For NAPKINS

MENU

Carpaccio, Arugula, and Parmesan Stacks

Herb and Onion Focaccia

Olives, Tomatoes, and Zucchini Red Sauce
over Fettuccine

Tiramisù Piled High

okay . . . picture this. It's almost Halloween my freshman year

of college. Because I was known as the "artsy" one in my group, two of my friends decided to look to me for costume inspiration. We were going to a couple of really huge parties and we needed really good costumes. I agreed heartily while thinking to myself . . . *WHATEVER* . . . Halloween was more than four whole days away and my mind had about a zillion things going on. And anyway, how long could three Halloween costumes take?

Well . . . sure enough, the morning of October 31 arrived, and my friends met me outside the arts building. "Well . . . what's it gonna be, Katie . . . what are we going to be?"

Think fast, think fast, think fast, my mind was saying . . .

"Primary colors!" my mouth was saying. "We are each going to be one!" I'm sure it was something from class—who knew? Back to my room we tromped. I had from the arts

building to the dorm to figure it all out. I had some pretty good stuff for us. I had some foul-weather gear for one friend that gave us YELLOW. A full-length red raincoat (which my mother thought I must have for college) served as our RED and for me . . . well, I had my bright, well, GREEN (close enough to blue!) rain jacket—and yes, you guessed it; the girl from Michigan had a matching hat.

In we marched to the first party. We stood at the door and looked around. *Ugh!* I could see all the upperclassmen saying, "The color guard has arrived." There we were, RED, YELLOW, and me—GREEN—amid a sea of girls complete with body paint, fishnets, French maid getups, and *anything* black. A freshman's nightmare!

We decided to try the next party. It was across campus, which was a hike! It started to pour about halfway there—and

wouldn't you know . . . we didn't get wet at all. By the time everybody else arrived . . . well, let's just say that body paint doesn't look so grand after a rainstorm and fishnets and heels don't really make it so well across campus. We were good to go! Now, amid the fishnets and body paint that was fading fast . . . well, I must admit; everybody thought we were pretty cool.

By two a.m., RED, YELLOW, and GREEN were home and starving and ready to rehash the best night of college yet! We sat on the floor of the dorm kitchen and heated up gobs of pasta with lots of sauce. The table surface was less than desirable to eat on, so I spread out my green rain jacket and that was our tablecloth. We chatted and laughed on into the dawn . . . what a night!

The inspiration for this table . . . well, what can I say—it sure worked for us!

Flag 'em Down

You Need

SUPPLIES

Brightly colored nylon fabric
Stitch witchery
White cotton canvas
Grommets
Colored paper
Laminate paper
Colorful string

TOOLS

Iron, Ironing board
Scissors
Grommet punch
Label printing machine
Hole punch

Get Started

THE FLAG

1. Cut nylon fabric into 18 x 12½-inch rectangles.
2. Using stitch witchery, hem the edges of the fabric approximately ¼ inch all the way around.
3. Cut the white canvas into a 4 x 12½-inch strip and hem all the edges.
4. Fold canvas fabric in half the long way over one short side of the nylon rectangle and attach with stitch witchery with the iron.
5. Attach grommets at both ends of the white canvas strip.

THE NAME TAG

1. Make name cards by printing your guest's name on a clear label and sticking it on a piece of brightly colored paper.
2. Laminate the name area and cut it out into a pennant shape.
3. Punch a hole on the long edge in the center to thread the string.
4. Tie the name tags to the grommet holes using brightly colored string.
5. Leave one of the tails about 8 to 10 inches long and allow the string to flow onto the tabletop.

Hints and Clues

You can also order banners and flags from a local store or mix and match old flags and banners.

Colored Ponds

Get Started

1. Fill glass bowls with water and add several drops of food coloring to achieve a vibrant color. Stir.
2. Cut off heads of flowers and float them in the bowls.

Hints and Clues

Food coloring will not hurt your flowers, although their color may be slightly affected.

You Need

SUPPLIES
Collection of low glass bowls
Food coloring
Flower blooms

TOOLS
Spoon
Garden clippers

Paint the Town Red

You Need

SUPPLIES

Thermo-hardening colored
paint
Clear glass dinner plates
Clear glasses

TOOLS

Paintbrush

Get Started

1. Paint different freehand shapes and designs on each plate and glass to make a unique set.

2. Allow painted pieces to dry for 24 hours.

3. Follow the instructions from the paint you've chosen. Most permanent color needs to be baked for 45 minutes to an hour at 325°F.

Hints and Clues

This is a great project to do with kids.

We like clear glass so that you can see the vibrant green tablecloth underneath, but feel free to use any plates you have.

Green Means Go

Get Started

1. Cover door with green fabric.

2. Wrap the fabric tightly around the edges of the door and staple it on the underside, creating a tightly wrapped tabletop.

3. Place Plexiglas on top of fabric-covered door and place brackets on the 4 corners.

4. Predrill holes where the screws for the brackets will go.

5. Screw corner brackets through the Plexiglas and the fabric and into the door.

Hints and Clues

Using an interior door for this tabletop is great because they are lightweight, inexpensive, and easy to hammer into, but if you can't get a door, plywood also works well.

If you can't find brightly colored fabric, paper can also be used for covering the tabletop.

Plexiglas usually comes with a thin plastic sheet coating on both sides since it scratches easily, so wait to remove the coating until the last minute!

Plexiglas is a plastic substitute for glass. It is lighter, thinner, and does not shatter.

You Need

SUPPLIES

Interior hollow-core door

Bright green fabric

Plexiglas cut to size

Oversize corner brackets

TOOLS

Staple gun/staples

Drill

Screwdriver, screws

Ready . . . Dip . . . Go!

You Need

SUPPLIES
Bright yellow marine paint
Clear glass bottles
Silver wire
Gerbera daisies

TOOLS
Disposable plastic bucket
Wire cutters

Get Started

1. Pour the yellow paint into a disposable bucket.
2. Dip and spin the bottles up to where the neck begins. The paint edge looks nice with a wavelike pattern rather than a straight line all the way around. Allow bottles to dry and repeat.
3. Group 3 bottles together and wrap them several times with silver wire, then twist wire together.
4. Fill the bottles with water and place the gerbera daisies in the bottles.

Hints and Clues
We like bottles grouped in threes, but feel free to combine groups of any number.

Watch out for gerbera daisies with tubes wrapped around the stems. They are most often wrapped too tightly and they can choke the stems off from water so the flowers don't last long; look for stems held up with wire, not tubes!

Sea Legs

Keep your eye out for sales on marine paint . . . it's cheapest in the summer/warm months, when the boats are in the water. The price goes up in the fall when the boats come out of the water for maintenance, so stock up if you see a good price! I discovered how great boat paint looks on furniture in my first apartment in New York. I came home from work to find that Kitty (my roommate) had treated all of our mismatched chairs to a bright blue coat and I couldn't believe my eyes. A transformation . . . they looked all grown-up!

You Need

SUPPLIES

Wooden chairs

Bright yellow marine paint

Table in need of a facelift

TOOLS

Sandpaper

Disposable paintbrushes

Disposable paint pan

Get Started

THE CHAIRS

1. Clean and sand the chairs.

2. Paint them with 2 coats of marine paint.

THE TABLE

1. Clean and sand the table.

2. Paint the legs and edge of the table with marine paint.

3. From the previous project, place the plywood or door on the top of the tabletop.

Hints and Clues

This is a great project to take mix and matched chairs and turn them into a complete set — once they are all the same bright, shiny color, nobody will notice that they started out differently. Be aware — this paint is waterproof, very thick, and should be used in a well-ventilated area. It's a good idea to use a drop cloth whenever you are painting.

Allow marine paint ample time to dry before applying a second coat.

Napkins to Dye For

Get Started

1. Fill bin with enough hot water to cover the fabric entirely. Follow the amount instructions that are given with the fabric dye you've chosen.
2. Wet your fabric with cold water before dyeing.
3. Agitate napkins constantly until the desired color is achieved.
4. Rinse napkins in warm and then in cold water to set the dye.
5. Hang to dry. Press napkins when dry.

Hints and Clues

This is a great project to recycle those old napkins with stains that you can't get out or to complete incomplete sets of napkins.

It does not matter what shade of white you start out with, as you are dyeing them all in the same color.

You might want to make the color stronger than you think you need, because it will fade somewhat as it dries.

You Need

SUPPLIES
Light-colored cotton napkins
Fabric dye

TOOLS
Bin
Spoon
Protective gloves
Drying rack

Did you know that all food coloring is highly concentrated? Be careful or your red could turn into maroon or brown!

Carpaccio, Arugula, and Parmesan Stacks

....

You Need

INGREDIENTS	AMOUNTS
Mayonnaise	¼ cup
Lemon juice	2 tablespoons
Dijon mustard	2 tablespoons
Salt	½ teaspoon
Cracked black pepper	½ teaspoon
Carpaccio (paper-thin slices of beef tenderloin)	16 slices
Arugula	1 bunch, washed, dried, and roughly chopped
Parmesan cheese	¼ pound, shaved

Get Cookin'

1. Make the mayonnaise sauce by mixing the mayonnaise, lemon juice, and mustard with a whisk.
2. Season with salt and pepper and set aside.
3. Lay in a slice of carpaccio, using a 2-inch length of 3-inch pipe as a mold, folding in the sides to fit in the mold.
4. Place a mound of chopped arugula on top of the carpaccio and then place another piece of carpaccio on top, folding over to fit in the pipe.
5. Pull off the pipe and top the stack with shaved Parmesan and fresh cracked pepper.
6. Drizzle with mayonnaise sauce.

Hints and Clues

Carpaccio is thinly sliced beef tenderloin, but you can also have a carpaccio of any type of meat that is safe to eat raw or cured (such as bison, boar, or duck) or high-quality fish.

Ask your butcher to prepare the carpaccio for you if you are interested.

Arugula has a peppery flavor that goes well with the salty Parmesan and tangy taste of lemon, mustard, and mayonnaise.

Use a flat vegetable peeler to shave Parmesan cheese. Use the peeler like you're peeling a carrot or cucumber to make thin shaved strips.

It is common to coat carpaccio with lemon juice and olive oil before serving it. They not only help to bring out the taste, but help with freshness and color.

Carpaccio is thinly shaved raw beef generally served as an appetizer. Although that seems simple enough, do not try to make it yourself. The meat must be very fresh and cut with a specially sanitized blade. Look for carpaccio at specialty food shops and Italian food markets. Or ask a butcher you trust to prepare some for you. It is not worth risking improper preparation!

Focaccia is a porous, nonflaky but crusty bread from Italy. It is very "in" now due to the relative ease of preparation—and you can really put anything you want on it . . . it can be a whole meal!

Herb and Onion Focaccia

You Need

INGREDIENTS	AMOUNTS
Pillsbury Pizza Dough	1 package (10 ounces)
Rosemary	2 tablespoons, finely chopped
Thyme	2 tablespoons, chopped
Olive oil	2 tablespoons
Red onion	1, julienned
Parmesan cheese	2 tablespoons, grated
Salt and pepper to taste	
Extra-virgin olive oil	Enough for drizzling

Get Cookin'

1. Preheat oven to 425°F.
2. Unroll the pizza dough as directed on the package onto a parchment-lined cookie sheet. Sprinkle half of the herbs on the dough and fold the dough in half lengthwise.
3. Brush the top with olive oil and evenly distribute the remaining herbs, onion, and cheese.
4. Salt and pepper to taste.
5. Bake for 15 minutes until the foccacia is golden brown and crispy.
6. Drizzle with extra-virgin olive oil and serve sliced.

Hints and Clues

You can use a pizza stone or pizza pan if you have one. Make sure the pan is heated in the oven thirty minutes before you put the dough on it.

Olives, Tomatoes, and Zucchini Red Sauce over Fettuccine

You Need

INGREDIENTS	AMOUNTS
Onion	¾ cup yellow, diced
Garlic cloves	2, thinly sliced
Canned whole tomatoes in juice	2 cups
Dried parsley	1 tablespoon
Dried sweet basil	1 tablespoon
Red wine	½ cup
Roma tomatoes	3 cups, diced (medium)
Zucchini	2 cups, diced (small-medium)
Black olives	1 cup, pitted and roughly chopped
Fresh parsley	3 tablespoons, chopped
Fresh basil	3 tablespoons, sliced in thin strips
Salt	to taste
Black pepper	½ teaspoon
Fettuccine	2 boxes (12 ounces)
GARNISH	
Parsley	3 or 4 sprigs
Grated Parmesan cheese to taste	

Get Cookin'

SAUCE

1. Over medium heat, cook the onion and garlic until soft, about 4 minutes.
2. Add the canned tomatoes with juice, dried parsley, and dried sweet basil and cook another 10 minutes.
3. Puree the sauce using a blender or food processor and return to heat.
4. Add the wine, the chopped fresh tomatoes, and zucchini and simmer for 10 minutes.
5. Finish by stirring in the pitted olives, fresh parsley, and fresh basil.
6. Season with 1½ teaspoons salt and the pepper.

PASTA

7. Boil about 4 cups of water with 1 tablespoon of salt.

8. Add the fettuccine and cook as directed on the package.

9. Drain the noodles, toss lightly in about 1 cup of the sauce, and then top with the remaining sauce.

10. Garnish with parsley sprigs and Parmesan cheese.

Hints and Clues

If sauce is too thick, add water to thin it out a little.

Always stir in fresh herbs at the end because they will brown if cooked for too long.

Tiramisù Piled High

....

You Need

INGREDIENTS	AMOUNTS
Eggs	3, separated
Granulated sugar	⅓ cup
Mascarpone cheese	1 cup
Espresso	¾ cup, instant brewed type
Marsala wine	½ cup
Store-bought chocolate sauce	At least 1 cup
Heavy cream	2 cups (1 pint)
Vanilla	1 tablespoon
Powdered sugar	2 tablespoons
Ladyfingers	24
Shaved bittersweet chocolate	¼ cup

Get Cookin'

ZABAGLIONE

1. In a double boiler, beat together the egg yolks and granulated sugar until creamy.
2. Add the mascarpone and 3 ounces of brewed espresso and simmer until thick.
3. Let cool.
4. Beat the egg whites until stiff and fold into the zabaglione.
5. Mix in the remaining coffee and the marsala.

CHOCOLATE

6. Heat the chocolate dipping sauce and set aside.

WHIPPED CREAM

7. Whip the heavy cream by hand or with an electric mixer until stiff.
8. Whip in the vanilla and powdered sugar.

ASSEMBLY

9. Dip 3 of the ladyfingers, one at a time, into the chocolate sauce and arrange in a single layer side by side on the plate.

10. Dip 2 ladyfingers in the cream sauce and arrange on top of the chocolate layer at an angle crossing the chocolate ladyfingers.

11. Cover with a layer of whipped cream and sprinkle on the chocolate shavings. You have just created one serving.

12. Refrigerate for 2 hours and serve.

13. Repeat the process for as many portions as you need.

Hints and Clues

By making the zabaglione in a double boiler, you are reducing the possibility of overcooking the eggs. Continue stirring the sugar and eggs during cooking.

Use a vegetable peeler to get shaved curls of chocolate.

10

Kitchen Garden

A LUNCH FOR FOUR

MENU

Soft Scrambled Eggs
 with Goat Cheese and Chives
Savory Scallion and Cayenne Scones
Sautéed Spring Spinach
Skewered Poached Salmon
Zesty Lemonies

PROJECTS

Stamp It! TABLE

Herbal Wrap NAPKIN RINGS

A Run of Dish Towels RUNNER

Spoon Soap FAVORS

It's a Wrap! WREATH

High Stakes CENTERPIECE

i've always loved to grow little herb gardens

in my window boxes, inside and out. Just put 'em in the soil and they grow and grow; it's amazing. I usually try to use my own homegrown herbs in cooking . . . a pinch here and a pinch there. Sometimes I use dried spices, especially when I am really busy! But when I was little, I saw the real thing.

Mrs. Brewster, our next-door neighbor, was an older lady. She lived in the house that had once belonged to her mother, and her mother's family before that. The house was always spotless and painted every other year, but beyond that I don't think there had been too many changes since her grandmother lived there. In fact, Mrs. Brewster herself was somewhat ageless. I have no idea how long her hair was because it was always in a bun. Always. She wore gold-rimmed spectacles. Every day she wore a long floral dress, and sometimes they were

the same pattern as my mother's wallpaper. This intrigued me even more.

In Mrs. Brewster's kitchen, there was a small door that led to a fenced-in garden only accessible from the kitchen. It was totally amazing. Of course she grew her own herbs, but her kitchen garden went beyond that. She grew carrots, radishes, rhubarb, and even asparagus. (Did you know that asparagus grow right out of the ground?) All through the summer and fall she picked and pruned, pickled and preserved.

Sometimes when my parents went out they would bring my sisters and me over to Mrs. Brewster's so she could "watch" us, but it was we who were doing a lot of the watching—of her! It was a totally different world over there. No television, no radio; Mrs. Brewster had board games with wooden pieces and books and dolls with the faces painted on. We were all experts pretty soon. We also

helped in the garden. Mostly we tied and dried, helping to preserve the herbs for winter and filling the house with wonderful scents.

One afternoon, Mrs. Brewster shared with us the fruits of her labor. It was late fall and the garden was in full bloom. She placed a wooden farm table over the empty patch in the garden and covered it with handmade towels. Then she laid this garden bounty around the edges of the table. I'll never forget the four of us sitting right in the center of Mrs. Brewster's tabletop kitchen garden . . . what a time we had!

In today's world, not many of us have the time to create our own full-size kitchen gardens. But there is always time to grow some herbs here and there. They add so much to any table and any home. While we can't all be Mrs. Brewster, sometimes it can be fun to try!

Stamp It!

You Need

SUPPLIES
Foam rubber mouse pad
Sanding plane with a handle
Oil base paint

TOOLS
Scissors or utility knife
Hot glue gun
Flat paint tray

Get Started

MAKING THE PATTERN
1. Sketch or trace the image you've chosen for your stamp onto a mousepad. (We chose a daisy motif.)
2. Cut the pattern from the mouse pad using scissors or a utility knife.

MAKING THE STAMP PAD
1. Cut a piece of mouse pad to cover the face of the sanding plane.
2. Glue the piece to the plane using the hot glue gun.
3. Attach the patterns to the base using the hot glue gun, creating the complete stamp pad.

STAMPING
1. Pour paint into a flat tray.
2. Press stamp into paint.
3. Press stamp onto the side of the table, applying firm and even pressure for a crisp impression with clean borders.
4. Continue the stamping process around the side of the table.

Hints and Clues
Stamps can be used in either direction to create a different look. Make sure you buy a sanding plane big enough for your pattern. It's a good idea to press out extra paint from the stamp to keep the image crisp. A great way to do this is to stamp a few times on scrap paper before you stamp the edge.

Did you know before it was so easy to photocopy things, large rubber stamps used to be used for forms and all sorts of other documents . . . kind of a precursor to the copy machine! Now they are collectibles.

Herbal Wrap

You Need

SUPPLIES

Fresh rosemary
(the longest pieces
you can find!)
Wooden clothespins

*Did you know that in
ancient Greece stu-
dents put a sprig of
rosemary in their hair,
as it was believed that
it strengthened and
stimulated memory?*

Get Started

1. Loosely braid three rosemary stems. The braid should be approximately 1 foot long.
2. Wrap the braid into a circle.
3. Clip both ends of the braid together with a clothespin.
4. Push napkin through napkin ring.

Hints and Clues

It's possible to choose other herbs for your napkin rings such as parsley or dill.

Only long-stemmed herbs are suitable for braiding.

A Run of Dish Towels

You Need

SUPPLIES
Dish towels
Wooden clothespins

When I was a kid, my mother told me I was the best dish dryer in the house! After proudly drying for years, thinking I had a special skill, I found out that anybody drying the dishes was the best to my mom.

Get Started

1. Place dish towels down the center of the table, overlapping them at the edges approximately 3 inches.
2. Repeat this process across the width of the table, creating a cross.
3. Connect the towels with clothespins at all overlapping points.

Hints and Clues

A variety of colors and patterns will create a fun, festive tabletop.

Spoon Soap

....

Get Started

1. Write the name of each guest on handles of the spoons or ladles.
2. Stir a tablespoon of either herb into the liquid glycerin soap.
3. Fill the jelly jars with soap and close lids.
4. Tie a piece of twine around the rim of the lid.
5. Insert spoon between twine and lid.

Hints and Clues

Make sure you instruct your guest to shake the jar well before using so that the herbal infusion permeates the whole jar. The herbs will tend to settle on the bottom otherwise.

Keep in mind you want approximately 1 cup of glycerin soap to 1 tablespoon fresh dried herbs.

You Need

SUPPLIES

Wooden spoons or ladles

Fresh dried chamomile

Fresh dried lavender

Liquid glycerin soap

Jelly jars

Twine

TOOLS

Sharpie

Scissors

It's a Wrap!

You Need

SUPPLIES

Dish towels

12-inch foam wreaths

Wooden clothespins

Small potted herbs, 2 inches in diameter

TOOLS

Pinking shears

Hot glue gun

Get Started

MAKING THE WREATH

1. Roll two dish towels from corner to corner.

2. Wrap each dish towel around one half of the wreath, covering the wreath completely.

3. Pin the towels together with a clothespin on both sides of the wreath where they meet.

CREATING THE POCKET

1. Cut a square from another dish towel.

2. Create the pocket by attaching three sides of the square to the wreath using a hot glue gun.

3. Place the potted herb into the pocket.

4. Hang a wreath on the back of each guest chair.

Hints and Clues

You can fill the pocket on your wreath with other kitchen items, like a small whisk or a jar of spice.

Hang the wreath on the back of a chair, in a kitchen window, or on your kitchen door.

High Stakes

Get Started

WIRE STAKES

1. Cut six 18-inch lengths of galvanized wire.

2. Wrap the piece of wire around a pencil about three times in the middle of the wire and at the top of the wire, leaving a small tail at the top.

NAME CARDS

1. Cut the card stock into small rectangles.

2. Write the name of the herbs and any pertinent or interesting information about them on the rectangles.

3. Slide the cards between the loops formed at the top of each stake.

POTTED HERBS

1. Tie a dish towel around each pot.

2. Put appropriate stakes in herbs.

Hints and Clues

You can make and use these stakes for different purposes on your table or in the kitchen.

Keep your eye out for vintage wire milk bottle caddies. We put the potted herbs in them for our centerpiece. I always find tons of things to do with them!

You Need

SUPPLIES

Galvanized wire

Heavy card stock

5-inch terra-cotta pots

6 potted herbs (parsley, thyme, sage, oregano, rosemary, dill)

6 dish towels

TOOLS

Wire cutters

Scissors

Pencil

Soft Scrambled Eggs with Goat Cheese and Chives

You Need

INGREDIENTS	AMOUNTS
Large eggs	10
Salt and pepper to taste	
Butter	1 tablespoon
Soft goat cheese	3 ounces, crumbled
Chives	¼ cup, thinly sliced on the bias

Get Cookin'

1. Beat the eggs and salt and pepper in a medium bowl.

2. In a medium nonstick skillet, melt the butter and coat the entire bottom of the pan. Add the eggs and cook over low heat, stirring constantly with a rubber spatula.

3. When the eggs start to set up, add the crumbled goat cheese and stir.

4. Add the chopped chives.

5. Serve immediately.

Hints and Clues

Cooking eggs over low heat and stirring them gently makes for softer, fluffier scrambled eggs. You can use a rubber spatula, fork, whisk, or wooden spoon to stir the eggs—but you need to be careful about scratching the nonstick pan.

Try alternating the color of eggs you buy; brown one week, white the next. That way, you'll never be confused about which eggs to use up first!

Savory Scallion and Cayenne Scones

You Need

INGREDIENTS	AMOUNTS
Flour	2 cups
Sugar	1 tablespoon
Baking powder	½ teaspoon
Salt	1½ teaspoons
Cayenne pepper	¾ teaspoon
Heavy cream	¾ cup
Sour cream	¼ cup
Scallions	4 tablespoons, thinly sliced
Butter	1 tablespoon, melted

Get Cookin'

1. Preheat the oven to 425°F.

2. In a large bowl or Kitchen Aid mixer, whisk the flour, sugar, baking powder, salt, and ½ teaspoon of cayenne pepper together.

3. Blend in the heavy cream and sour cream until a dough forms and it is evenly moistened.

4. Stir in 2 tablespoons of scallions.

5. Gather the dough together in a ball and knead gently 4 or 5 times.

6. On a lightly floured surface, roll the dough into a round that is ¾ inch thick.

7. Using a 2½-inch cookie cutter, cut out 8 rounds.

8. Transfer scones to a baking sheet and brush with the melted butter. Sprinkle scones with remaining cayenne and scallions.

9. Bake for 20 minutes, or until lightly browned.

Did you know that scones originated in Scotland? Their name came from the stone in front of which Scottish kings were crowned; called the scone, it looks like its food counterpart.

Sautéed Spring Spinach

You Need

INGREDIENTS	AMOUNTS
Fresh spring spinach	3 pounds
Olive oil	2 to 3 tablespoons
Salt and pepper to taste	
Nutmeg	a pinch

Get Cookin'

1. Trim and clean the spinach. Be sure to dry it thoroughly.
2. In a medium sauté pan over medium-low heat, heat the olive oil and add the spinach. Cook for 2 to 3 minutes, or until the spinach just starts to wilt.
3. Season with salt and pepper and nutmeg.
4. Serve immediately.

Spinach contains oxalic acid, which is a natural inhibitor of iron absorption. Translation: Although spinach contains a high amount of iron, only small amounts of it can be absorbed into the human body. Needless to say—the same is not true for cartoon characters!

Skewered Poached Salmon

You Need

INGREDIENTS	AMOUNTS
Water	4 cups
White wine	½ cup
Lemon	3 slices, ¼ inch thick
Black peppercorns	15 whole
Bay leaves	3
Carrots	¾ cup, diced
Celery	¾ cup, diced
Onions	½ cup, diced
Salmon	4 6-ounce fillets
Fresh dill	4 tablespoons, roughly chopped
Salt	2 teaspoons
Pepper	fresh cracked, to taste

Did you know that the Chinook or "King" salmon can reach up to 120 pounds? That's a big fish!

Get Cookin'

1. Place all the ingredients except the salmon, dill, salt, and pepper in a saucepan and cover.
2. Bring to a boil.
3. Reduce heat and simmer for 30 minutes.
4. Season the salmon fillets with dill, salt, and pepper.
5. Cut the seasoned fillets into cubes and place on the skewers (about 3 pieces on each skewer).
6. When the court bouillon is ready, reduce heat to low and place the salmon skewers in the pot with the court bouillon.
7. Cover and cook for 2 minutes.
8. Remove from the liquid and serve.

Hints and Clues

Do not cube the fish until you are ready to cook it; whole pieces of fish will stay fresh longer.
We recommend using wooden skewers that are approximately 5 inches long.

Zesty Lemonies

....

You Need

INGREDIENTS	AMOUNTS
CRUST	
Flour	1⅓ cups
Confectioners' sugar	¼ cup plus 2 tablespoons (for sifting on top)
Salt	2 teaspoons
Unsalted butter	11 tablespoons (1 stick plus 3 tablespoons), at room temperature
FILLING	
Eggs	6 large, beaten
Granulated sugar	2 cups
Salt	1 teaspoon
Lemon juice	⅓ cup
Lemon zest	4 teaspoons, grated
Flour	6 tablespoons
Baking powder	2 teaspoons

Get Cookin'

1. Preheat oven to 350°F.

CRUST

2. Butter an 11 x 7 x 1½-inch Pyrex dish.

3. In the bowl of a food processor, pulse together the flour, ¼ cup confectioners' sugar, and salt till well combined.

4. Pulse in the butter until the dough resembles coarse meal.

5. Press the mixture into the buttered Pyrex dish.

6. Bake for 20 to 25 minutes, or until lightly browned.

7. Let cool 10 to 15 minutes.

FILLING

8. In the bowl of an electric mixer, beat the eggs until blended.

9. Slowly add the granulated sugar and salt; continue beating.

10. Add the lemon juice and lemon zest into the egg mixture.

11. Sift the flour and baking powder. Add this to the egg mixture and blend.

12. Spread the mixture evenly over the crust and return to oven to bake for 25 to 30 minutes, or until golden brown on top and the bars look set.

13. Remove and let stand on a cooling rack until completely cooled.

14. Sift the remaining 2 tablespoons confectioners' sugar over the top.

15. Slice and serve.

Hints and Clues

Be sure to evenly press the dough into the baking dish.

Sift the dry ingredients so that no lumps develop in the filling.

11

Romance in the Morning

A BREAKFAST FOR TWO

PROJECTS

A Furniture Facial TABLE

Pushin' for a Cushion CHAIRS

Silver Lining NAPKINS

Best Dressed TABLE

Charming China PLATES

Pressing Posies PLACE MATS

Edible Elegance FAVORS

Sunrise and Sparkles NAPKIN RINGS AND SILVERWARE

Music in the Air LIGHTING

MENU

Challah French Toast
with Vanilla and Nutmeg

Spiced Poached Pears

Chocolate Truffles for Two

Shaved Ice Mimosas

when i was sixteen i got in big trouble.

I have no idea what I did. I don't even remember exactly what the punishment was, but what I *do* remember is that it was a big deal. Huge. I was banished to my room. What was I going to do for eternity stuck in the house?

Necessity being the mother of invention, I came up with my brilliant scheme: a romantic breakfast for my parents would surely make them forget my troubles. Problems arose immediately.

I started by secretly scavenging around the house for props. Within the first few minutes of my seemingly successful hunt, my mother demanded to know what I was doing with her grandmother's rose pink Limoges and the candlesticks from the dining room table. This wasn't going to be as easy as I thought.

Back to my room I went.

My options now severely limited, I threw myself onto my bean bag. I must have been looking upward for some sort of teenage divine intervention when I noticed the attic trapdoor looking back at me. There had to be stuff up there I could use!

A quick trip yielded many possibilities. Some old drapes here, a few flowery pillows there, and the greatest little table with all the paint peeling off (*the perfect look!*), and 2 chairs set my mind to work. My fortunes appeared to be improving.

When my parents were finally asleep, I crept out of my bed and set out to the task. By that point I was completely sure that both my parents would be swept off their feet.

My table turned out to look somewhat like this one, although I must admit that time and testing have improved upon the original.

As for my parents . . . my father noticed a light under my door at around 4:30 a.m. and decided not only to see what was going on in my room, but to wake my mother so she could come, too. They found me slumped over my romantic table for two asleep and still definitely very much in trouble.

A Furniture Facial

You Need

SUPPLIES
Paint and varnish remover
Wooden table in need
of a facelift
Soap
Paper towels or rags

TOOLS
Heavy-duty utility gloves
Natural bristle brush
Flexible metal scraper
Steel wool

Keep your eye out for wooden tables and chairs that already have several coats of paint for easier distressing. The fun of stripping an old piece of furniture is discovering its history as the layers reveal themselves.

Get Started

1. Apply a thick layer of paint remover to surface with a brush. Remember to brush in one direction only!
2. Scrape paint when it starts to bubble.
3. Reapply remover and scrape until you get the look you want.
4. Wash surface with soap and water and wipe dry.

Hints and Clues

Use paint remover in well-ventilated area or outdoors if possible.

Always use natural bristle brushes when applying paint remover. Paint remover can melt synthetic bristles!

Use steel wool to remove paint from cracks and grooves or if finish needs smoothing.

As various layers of paint begin to peek through, you may choose not to completely strip your piece, leaving different shades and colors that add extra interest.

Pushin' for a Cushion

Get Started

1. Put pillow evenly over the seat of the chair with all ruffled or flange edges falling over the edge of the chair seat.

2. Cut ribbon into 8-inch-long pieces.

3. Fold each piece in half.

4. Fold the halves again, leaving one flap longer than the rest on each piece.

5. Trim the longer flap end into an upside-down *V*.

6. Hammer upholstery tacks through the edges of the pillow and ribbon into the edges of the chair every few inches or as needed.

7. Continue adjusting the pillow as you attach it to the chair for a smoother look.

Hints and Clues

Test your pillow for height and comfort before attaching it to the chair. If pillow seat is too high for the table, remove filler and replace with batting or thinner filler. Upholstery tacks make noticeable holes in fabric, so place them with care!

Before the 1970s upholstery tacks were available only to tradespeople. Since then, the availability of the tacks has increased as more and more amateurs upholster their own furniture. Upholstery tacks come in a variety of sizes and shapes. The typical tack has a steel-filled head, but they can also be made from solid brass and copper. They differ from regular thumbtacks in shape, looks, and—most of all—strength.

You Need

SUPPLIES

2 floral pillows with floppy
    edges (approximately the
    same size as the chair seats)
2 distressed chairs
Ribbon
Upholstery tacks

TOOLS

Scissors
Hammer

Silver Lining

You Need

SUPPLIES
Vintage curtains
Damask fabric
Self-adhesive Velcro

TOOLS
Ruler
Pinking shears
Iron
Ironing board

Keep your eye out for vintage curtains or drapes, which are easily stored for later use!

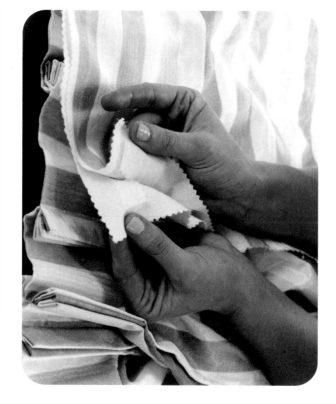

Get Started

1. Put curtain face down on flat surface and lay damask fabric face up on top of curtain.

2. Measure and mark two 18-inch squares.

3. Cut squares with pinking shears, making sure to cut through both layers.

4. Iron the fabric.

5. Adhere 1-inch strips of Velcro at each corner between the layers of fabric and attach the two pieces together.

Hints and Clues

This is a great way to use old drapes.

Washcloths also make — great napkin liners.

Best Dressed

You Need

SUPPLIES

Fringe

Table

TOOLS

Hot glue gun

Scissors

Keep your eye out for silk or satin fringe remnants that are long enough to wrap around the edge of a table.

Get Started

1. Starting in a corner, attach fringe to the inside edge of the table using the glue gun. Try to use a single piece of fringe all the way around. Glue trim a few inches at a time, letting glue dry before starting on next few inches.

2. Cut fringe where fringe ends meet at the starting point.

Hints and Clues

If the table does not have a dropped edge, you can attach the trim to the outside edge of tabletop.

Charming China

SUPPLIES

Sheet music

Clear dinner plates

Flower petals

The first time I was supposed to play from a piece of sheet music was also my first public appearance, the fifth grade recital. It took place at our local music store. When the time came for me to take my seat at the piano, I was so nervous that I couldn't make my hands move. Several minutes that seemed like hours passed. Finally I got up from my seat, hung my head, and walked offstage. I guess that was the end of my stage fright!

Get Started

1. Place a sheet of music on a clear plate.

2. Trim the sheet music so that it is the same size as the plate.

3. Scatter fresh petals across the top of the sheet music.

4. Place another clear plate over the top.

Hints and Clues

Place a love note between your plates instead of sheet music.

Pressing Posies

Get Started

1. Unclip and separate Plexiglas.
2. Put one piece of Plexiglas on a flat surface.
3. Arrange flowers on Plexiglas as desired.
4. Reattach the top sheet of the frame.

Hints and Clues

Make sure you will be able to see the majority of the flowers once the plate is placed on the mat.

Daisies, pansies, and dahlias press well. Look for flat, open flowers rather than tall, closed flowers like roses.

Prepress flowers in a book to create a flatter surface when you place the flowers on the Plexiglas. Prepressing flowers also eliminates discharge.

You Need

SUPPLIES

Clear, double-sided
16 x 20-inch Plexiglas frames
Fresh flowers

Edible Elegance

You Need

SUPPLIES

Rose petals or other edible
flowers

Egg white

Extra-fine sugar

TOOLS

Paper towels

Whisk

Small bowl

Small paintbrush

Wax paper

Did you know that everyday dandelions are edible? Just make sure no bees are near!

Get Started

1. Gently rinse petals in cool water.

2. Place wet petals on paper towels and air dry or gently blot dry.

3. Whisk egg white in a small bowl until foamy.

4. Dip brush in egg white and lightly brush side of each petal with a thin coat.

5. Sprinkle petals lightly with sugar while petals are still moist.

6. Lay coated petals on wax paper and allow them to dry completely.

Hints and Clues

Edible flowers include daylilies, geraniums, pansies, roses, begonias, and violets—
organically grown, of course, for safer eating.

Store candied petals in a tightly covered container for up to a week.

Sunrise and Sparkles

Get Started

1. Cut a piece of wire for each piece of silverware and napkin ring approximately 12 inches in length.

2. String approximately 7½ inches of beads onto each wire.

3. For silverware, connect the wire to the silverware by wrapping it around the neck of the utensil. Align the already strung beads down the center of the handle and wrap the end piece of wire around the end of the handle.

4. For napkin rings, make rings out of the beaded wire and seal the rings by twisting the ends.

Hints and Clues

String beads of various sizes and patterns for variety. Make each piece of gem wrap a little different to create an eclectic tabletop. Why not use your favorite costume necklace that has come unstrung for this project?

Surprisingly affordable, antique flatware is often sold from big bins at swap meets, antiques markets, and flea markets. If you are patient, pick one pattern and collect silverware until you have a full set.

Keep your eye out for glass beads with holes already drilled through (always check stones and beads for chips).

You Need

SUPPLIES

Thin silver wire

Large clear beads

TOOLS

Wire cutters

Music in the Air

You Need

SUPPLIES

4½-inch terra-cotta pot

Sand

Sheet music

3½ x 5½-inch
off-white pillar candle

Flower petals

Vintage astrid crystals

TOOLS

Transparent tape

Get Started

1. Fill bottom of pot with about 2 inches of sand.

2. Make 3 cones from sheet music, placing one over the other to create 3 layers. Secure with tape.

3. Put sheet music cone in pot, with the point in the sand.

4. Put candle into cone, anchoring as tightly as possible.

5. Rip edges of music downward so that at least 2 inches of the candle is exposed.

6. Place flower petals between the paper and the candle, all the way around.

7. Hang astrids off top of pot.

Hints and Clues

Choose sheet music lyrics that are part of a special memory.

Warning: Do not leave this candle unattended; the paper may burn!

Astrids were very common in the Victorian era. They would hang off lamps and just about anywhere else a person could hang them! They are really prisms with holes and wires through them, cut into fancy shapes.

Challah French Toast with Vanilla and Nutmeg

You Need

INGREDIENTS	AMOUNTS
Milk	¾ cup
Eggs	3 large
Vanilla	1 teaspoon
Nutmeg	½ teaspoon
Orange juice	2 tablespoons
Salt	½ teaspoon
Challah bread	4 1-inch-thick slices cut into a heart shape
Butter	1 tablespoon

Get Cookin'

1. Whisk together the milk, eggs, vanilla, nutmeg, orange juice, and salt in a medium bowl.

2. Soak the bread slices in the mixture for approximately 1 minute each, flipping each piece to make sure both sides have absorbed liquid.

3. Heat butter over medium heat in a skillet until melted.

4. Add the bread and "fry" on each side for about 4 minutes until lightly brown.

5. Remove from heat and serve with warm pears and syrup (recipe follows).

Hints and Clues

Make the French toast into hearts by making a half heart shape with a piece of parchment paper. Using that as your guide, cut each slice of challah in a half heart and then serve 2 halves per serving, placed together on the plate to make a heart shape.

Challah is airy bread made with yeast and many eggs. It is traditional Jewish bread, always served on the Sabbath and holidays. It makes the best French toast, because it is so airy it soaks up the eggs. It is available at many bakeries and grocery stores.

Spiced Poached Pears

You Need

INGREDIENTS	AMOUNTS
Water	1 cup
Sugar	½ cup
Orange zest	3 strips
Whole cloves	7
Vanilla extract	1 teaspoon
Star anise	2
Raisins	¼ cup
Whole pears (Comice)	3, peeled and cored
Maple syrup	¾ cup

Get Cookin'

1. Bring water and sugar to a boil and then reduce to a simmer.

2. Add orange zest, cloves, vanilla, star anise, raisins, and pears.

3. Cook for about 15 minutes or until liquid starts to thicken (test pears with a skewer or knife for tenderness).

4. Remove pears.

5. Chop 2 pears into cubes or pulse in a food processor. Slice 1 pear in half and set aside for garnish.

6. Continue simmering the liquid, adding the maple syrup until the liquid has thickened.

7. Place the pears on top of the French toast and drizzle with the syrup.

Hints and Clues

Flavors of the orange peel, cloves, etc. are infused into the pears and liquid as they simmer.

Raisins will grow larger as they simmer.

Try vanilla beans for an additional garnish!

Did you know that pears are harvested in the fall months of September and October? Keep your eye out for pears that are firmer and slightly underripe because they are best for poaching.

Chocolate Truffles for Two

You Need

INGREDIENTS	AMOUNTS
Heavy cream	¼ cup
Semisweet chocolate	6 ounces, finely chopped
Butter	4 tablespoons, at room temperature
Vanilla extract	2 teaspoons
Dried cherries	⅓ cup, chopped
Baking cocoa	½ cup

Get Cookin'

1. Boil cream on low heat for about 3 minutes or until reduced to about 2 tablespoons.

2. Add chopped chocolate, return to low heat, and stir until chocolate is completely melted.

3. Whisk in the butter and vanilla extract until smooth.

4. Add the dried cherries.

5. Pour into a Pyrex loaf pan and refrigerate until hard (at least 1 hour).

6. Remove pan from refrigerator and let stand at room temperature for 10 to 15 minutes.

7. Scoop out chocolate with a teaspoon and roll it into ½-inch balls.

8. Roll truffles in cocoa powder.

9. Place in the refrigerator or freezer up until serving time.

Hints and Clues

Reroll the truffles in cocoa powder before serving.

Always use a teaspoon to scoop out the truffles.

Store on 2 parchment-lined sheet pan in refrigerator.

Shaved Ice Mimosas

You Need

INGREDIENTS	AMOUNTS
Orange juice	1 can frozen, made as directed, or 1 carton, chilled
Champagne	1 bottle, chilled
Strawberries	2

Get Cookin'

1. Fill an ice tray with orange juice and place in freezer.
2. When frozen, remove cubes from tray and shave the orange juice cubes with a knife to make orange ice. Place shaved ice in the bottom of the champagne glasses.
3. Fill each glass two-thirds full with chilled champagne.

4. Top off with orange juice and garnish with a strawberry.

Hints and Clues
If you don't want to use alcohol, you can substitute sparkling cider for the champagne.

Okay, I know usually mimosas are not served with ice, but they're only good when cold, so why not?

12

Thanksgiving

THE WAY IT SHOULD BE!

PROJECTS

Easel of Twigs PLACE CARDS

Pilgrim Pillars LIGHTING

Bird's Nest HEADDRESS

Pot Luck CENTERPIECE

Twists of Bounty NAPKIN RINGS

Peacock and Lemon Leaf Cornucopia PLATTER

Harvest Scroll MENU

Fall's Shawl CHAIR

Twig on Twig PLACE MATS

Fall Blanket TABLECLOTH

MENU

Roast Turkey

Walnut, Sausage, and Apple Stuffing

Smashed Red Skin Potatoes

Bacon-Tossed Brussels Sprouts

Orange Zest Cranberry Sauce

Parker House Rolls with

American Spoon Pumpkin Butter

Graham Cracker Crust Sweet Potato Pie

Cheddar Cheese Crust Apple Pie

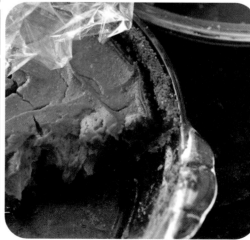

i really wanted to put a new twist on Thanksgiving.

I love tradition, but I thought Thanksgiving needed a kick in the pants. How could I make Thanksgiving more interesting? I tried a lot of different things at home. I watched television, and I read about other people's ideas. I came up with a lot of new ideas myself.

There were all sorts of different things I could make: turkey lasagna, turkey fritters, two chickens in lieu of one turkey, rock cornish hens—one whole bird to a person—or how about squab? Hmmm . . . that could be interesting.

I settled on the turkey lasagna.

I cooked and experimented and came up with what I thought was the perfect turkey lasagna. In fact, I ground the turkey meat myself! The sauce was great. And to get all the trimmin's in there . . . how about corn chips and cranberry corn chips. Right? What could be more original?

I took my new Thanksgiving recipe to the ultimate testing ground: home to my parents.

I brought the turkey lasagna out to the dining room where my father was standing . . . waiting to carve. I put the still-bubbling platter down in front of his place and handed him a spatula. What more could he need? I sat down.

You should have seen the look on my dad's face. He appeared to be in total shock . . . He was staring at me in complete amazement. "Katie, Katie, Katie . . . What is going on?" He did his best at cutting up and serving my creation, and we passed around the chips.

"Well . . . at least it smells good," was all I got from Dad.

In fact, it was good. We all had seconds. I got in my old bed that night and thought about Thanksgiving some more. Now, who has ever thought of turkey lasagna for

Thanksgiving? It was pretty original and it was darn good.

Then I thought of all the Thanksgivings I have spent with my family and what helped to make them special. It was all about the familiar smells, the familiar tastes and feels, and the beginning of the cold weather. It's about just the same thing as the year before and that's why everybody looks forward to it. It was about my father carving the bird—or at least having a bird at all. When I woke up, I knew my father was right.

Thanksgiving is about the harvest. It's about the stories we all learned when we were young. It's cranberry anything, potatoes, stuffing, the works! It's about a carving knife not a spatula. Thanksgiving creates a feeling I don't want to change. I'll give anyone my recipe for turkey lasagna anytime—except for Thanksgiving. It's turkey or bust.

Easel of Twigs

You Need

SUPPLIES
4-inch twigs (4 per easel)
Raffia
Card stock

TOOLS
Glue gun
Scissors
Sharpie

Did you know that raffia comes from the raffia palm, which is found in Madagascar?

Get Started

MAKING THE EASEL

1. Glue 3 twigs together in the shape of a triangle, leaving about 1 inch of twig overlapping on each of the three sides.

2. Stand the twigs upright and place a fourth twig on the backside, forming a teepee shape. (This fourth twig is used like a kick stand and completes the easel.)

3. Wrap small lengths of raffia around each of the areas that are glued together and tie with a knot.

MAKING THE NAME CARD

4. Cut the card stock down to name card size, about 1½ x 2-inch rectangles

5. Write your guests' name on the name cards.

6. Place each name card on an easel.

7. Put each place card at the appropriate place on the table.

Hints and Clues

The raffia can also cover up any glue that shows!

Pilgrim Pillars

Get Started

1. Brush a layer of silicon gel over both sides of the leaves, covering them completely.

2. Drill through the center of the chestnut using a small drill bit.
(You could use a nail and hammer to make a hole through the chestnut,
but make sure the chestnut is semisoft so it won't split.)

3. Spread 3 to 4 leaves into a fan with the tops of the leaves in different directions.

4. Center the leaves on the pillar candle.

5. Secure them with copper wire, circling the wire around the candle twice. (Leave enough room at the top for the candle to burn a few inches without hitting the leaves.)

6. Twist the wire together to hold, leaving approximately 5-inch-long tails.

7. String a chestnut onto one of the wire ends and slide it down onto the center of the leaves.

8. Pull the second tail over the outside of the chestnut and string it through.

9. Twist the wire tails together with needle-nose pliers to secure. (The twist should be small and delicate.)

Hints and Clues

Silicon gel is a heat-resistant material that protects the dry leaves from the heat of the flame.

Collect and press your fall leaves so that they become flat. You can keep them between layers of cardboard until you need them!

Leaf edges may still curl after pressing, but that adds depth and dimension to the design.

Warning: Do not leave unattended because heat-resistant material does not make it fireproof.

Look for antique flower and leaf presses at flea markets . . . nothing works like the old ones!

You Need

SUPPLIES

Clear silicon gel

Fall leaves

Chestnuts

Pillar candles, various sizes

Copper wire

TOOLS

Paintbrush

Drill and drill bits

Wire cutters

Needle-nose pliers

Bird's Nest

You Need

SUPPLIES

Grapevine wreath

Copper wire

Ceiling hook

Assortment of dried flowers

TOOLS

Wire cutters

Garden clippers

Get Started

MAKING THE NEST

1. Cut off the vine that holds the wreath together.

2. Stretch the bundle apart like an accordion, making sure that it stays in a circle, to desired length.

3. Run a copper wire from the bottom piece of grapevine, weaving in and out until you reach the top, leaving enough excess wire to hang the wreath from the ceiling hook.

4. Repeat process three more times, creating 4 wire strands to hang headdress from.

5. Bring the 4 wires together. Attach to a ceiling hook that should be centered over the table.

MAKING THE BOUQUETS

6. Make 4 to 5 bouquets from the dried flowers. Secure each bouquet with wire.

7. Randomly place bouquets in and around the bird's nest. Secure the bouquets in place with wire.

Hints and Clues

Sit at your table before hanging the headdress, to test for the perfect height for hanging!

> *I made this wreath for my New Year's Eve 2000 party and it was so much of a success I still haven't taken it down.*

Pot Luck

You Need

SUPPLIES

Collection of vintage tin
and cast-iron pots

Nuts

Preserved fruits

Fall leaves

Dried flower blossoms

Get Started

1. Place a selection of vintage cookware down the center of the table.

2. Randomly drop a mixture of nuts, preserved fruits, fall leaves, and dried flower blossoms into the cookware until the desired look is achieved.

Hints and Clues

You might be tempted to use potpourri, but the scents could ruin the aromas of your meal!

Keep your eye out for cast-iron pots at swap meets or in your grandmother's cupboard, but remember . . . all cast-iron pots have to be treated with oil before they can be used for cooking!

Twists of Bounty

You Need

SUPPLIES

Napkins
Small dried Indian corn
Copper wire
Preserved orange slices

TOOLS

Wire cutters
Needle-nose pliers

Get Started

1. Fold a napkin into the shape you would like to wrap.

2. Place the Indian corn on top of the napkin and secure it by wrapping it with copper wire.

3. Wrap the wire around the napkin several times making sure that the ends meet on top of the corn, leaving two 5-inch wire tails.

4. Place the preserved orange on top of the corn and string the copper wire through both sides of the orange.

5. Twist together with needle-nose pliers and cut off any excess wire.

Hints and Clues

Don't pull the wire too tightly around the napkin — you won't be able to pull the napkin out!

Peacock and Lemon Leaf Cornucopia

You Need

SUPPLIES
Peacock feathers

Wicker cornucopia

Lemon leaves

TOOLS
Glue gun

Clippers

Get Started

1. Attach the tops of the longest feathers around the mouth of the cornucopia with hot glue.

2. Clip off the quills of the feathers.

3. Starting directly under the "eye" of one feather in the top row, glue another row around the cornucopia.

4. Repeat the process until the top ¾ of the cornucopia is covered with rows of feathers.

5. Attach lemon leaves to the bottom ⅓ of the cornucopia with the hot glue gun.

6. Continue the gluing process until the bottom of the cornucopia is covered.

7. Trim excess glue strands.

Hints and Clues
Buy the feathers and leaves after you have chosen your cornucopia to be able to better estimate the amount needed.

Harvest Scroll

> *Did you know that birch bark is used to make canoes and that the sap from a birch tree can be used to patch a canoe?*

You Need

SUPPLIES

2 pieces of bark, 2½-feet
    long each
Preserved orange slices
Copper wire
Chestnuts
Heavy card stock

TOOLS

Awl
Wire cutters
Drill with small bit attachment
Sharpie

Get Started

1. Place the two pieces of bark on top of each other with the bark facing out on both sides.

2. Puncture a hole through both pieces of bark in the upper left-hand corner with an awl.

3. Repeat the process in the bottom right-hand corner.

4. Place the preserved orange slice over the holes and thread the copper wire through the seed holes, through both pieces of bark, and back through the orange slice, ending with both ends of the copper wire on the front of the orange.

5. Drill a hole through both sides of the chestnut using a small drill bit. You can also use a hammer and small nail or brad to make the hole.

6. Slide the drilled chestnut onto one of the copper wires and pull the second wire over the outside of the chestnut; join them together by twisting tightly.

7. Repeat the same process on the lower right-hand corner.

8. Write the menu on a piece of parchment paper or heavy card stock and slide it onto the scroll. It will rest in place.

Hints and Clues

We used Melaluca bark, which is thin and will curl up on the sides. It works as the base and will allow the bark to stand upright.

Fall's Shawl

You Need

SUPPLIES

4 feet of cheesecloth
approximately 8 inches wide
Dried fall leaves
Straw flowers on wire
(or dried blooms)

TOOLS

Ruler
Scissors
Wire cutters
Glue gun

Get Started

SHAWLING THE CHAIR

1. Measure the chair back to determine how long and how wide the cheesecloth shawl should be.

2. Cut the cheesecloth to size.

3. Tie the shawl around the chair back, leaving 2 equal tails.

DECORATING THE SHAWL

4. Spread 3 leaves into a fan.

5. Puncture the center of the stacked leaves with the wired flower, pulling the wire all the way through to create a decorative button.

6. Pierce the knot of the cheesecloth shawl with the decorative button.

7. Twist the wire around the knot to secure.

8. Cut off any excess wire.

Hints and Clues

We trimmed the tails of the cheesecloth for a more finished look.

If your decorative button needs to be held together better, use a dab of hot glue.

When I was a child we had Thanksgiving on Mackinac Island. Because there are no cars allowed on the island, a horse and carriage would pick us up at the airport and take us to our destination . . . talk about over the river and through the woods . . .

Twig on Twig

You Need

SUPPLIES
12-inch-long twigs, approximately 16 to 20 per mat

TOOLS
Glue gun
Garden clippers

Get Started

1. Place two 12-inch twigs parallel to each other in a vertical direction with 11 inches in between them.

2. Glue twigs horizontally from the top to the bottom of the vertical twigs, leaving about ½ inch of space between each branch.

3. Place 2 more vertical twigs on top of the horizontal branches on top of the bottom vertical branches, making a frame on two sides.

Hints and Clues

You may have strings of excess glue you need to trim from the mats.

Fall Blanket

Get Started

1. Spread a single layer of cheesecloth over the table like a tablecloth.

2. Scatter pressed leaves over the cheesecloth, creating the look of fallen leaves on a windy day.

3. Cover the leaves with another layer of cheesecloth.

4. Weave the quills of the feathers through the edges of the cheesecloth, holding the layers together.

5. Continue all the way around the circumference of the cloth.

Hints and Clues

If the cheesecloth is not wide enough to cover your table, you may need to use several strips to cover the width of the table.

When I lived in Los Angeles, I used to hang Michigan fall leaves from my ceiling from fishing line so that they rustled when I came in the door. I had the only fall day for miles!

You Need

SUPPLIES

Cheesecloth

Pressed fall leaves

White feathers

Roast Turkey

....

You Need

INGREDIENTS	AMOUNTS
Turkey, rinsed and dried	10 to 12 pounds
Lemons	3, cut in half
Parsley	10 whole sprigs
Onions	3, cut into ½-inch-thick rings
Carrots	4 to 5 whole
Celery	4 stalks
Butter	1 stick, melted

Get Cookin'

1. Preheat oven to 425°F.
2. Stuff cavity of turkey with halved lemons and parsley.
3. Tie the legs of the turkey together with kitchen string and tuck the wings behind the turkey neck.
4. Place the turkey in a roasting pan on a bed of the sliced onions, carrots, and celery stalks.
5. Cook for 30 minutes and then turn oven down to 350°F.
6. Baste with butter at least every hour until cooked through—internal temperature of 170°F for breast and 180°F for the thigh.

Hints and Clues

Before cooking, rinse the inside and outside of your turkey and pat dry.

If using a frozen turkey, allow 2 days for it to thaw in the refrigerator.

Turkey cooks at 15 to 20 minutes per pound; if stuffing your bird, add another 5 minutes per pound.

When the turkey is done the juices should run clear with no trace of pink.

Let your turkey stand for 15 minutes before carving. This allows the juices to return to the meat.

Walnut, Sausage, and Apple Stuffing

....

You Need

INGREDIENTS	AMOUNTS
Celery	1½ cups, diced ½ inch
Shallots	1 cup, diced ½ inch
Butter	2 tablespoons plus 6 tablespoons, melted
Italian sausage (links)	1½ pounds
Walnuts	1¼ cups
Granny Smith apples	2 cups, peeled and diced ½ inch
Parsley	¼ cup, minced
Rosemary	¼ cup, minced
Sage	¼ cup, minced
Bread stuffing, herbed and cubed	6 cups
Low-sodium chicken broth	2 cups, warm
Salt and pepper to taste	

Get Cookin'

1. Preheat oven to 325°F.

2. Over low to medium heat, cook the shallots and celery together, covered, in a sauté pan with 2 tablespoons of butter.

3. Transfer to a large bowl when they are softened, about 7 minutes.

4. Cook the sausage in the same pan and make sure the sausage is cooked through, around 10 minutes.

5. Slice sausage in ¼-inch rounds and then transfer to the same bowl with the celery and shallots.

6. Toast the walnuts on a cookie sheet until brittle but not burnt, about 10 minutes at 325°F.

7. Roughly chop walnuts and add to the bowl.

8. Cut the peeled apples into cubes and add to the bowl with the other ingredients.

9. Add the minced herbs to the bowl and mix.

10. Add the bread stuffing and toss to mix all the ingredients.

11. Add the warm chicken broth and the melted butter and mix thoroughly, making sure the bread is well coated.

12. Put the stuffing in a buttered casserole dish and cover with foil.

13. Bake for 30 minutes, covered, and then remove foil and bake for another 10 minutes, uncovered.

Hints and Clues

Make sure the bread crumbs are well coated with the chicken broth and butter before baking, to ensure that the stuffing does not turn out dry.

If you have difficulty finding shallots, you can substitute red, yellow, or white onions.

Smashed Red Skin Potatoes

You Need

INGREDIENTS	AMOUNTS
New red potatoes	15 to 20, chopped, with skin on
Heavy cream	¾ cup
Unsalted butter	1 stick (8 tablespoons)
Sour cream	½ cup
Salt and pepper to taste	

Get Cookin'

1. Place the potatoes in a large saucepan, add water to cover, and heat to boiling. Make sure you salt the water to add flavor to the potatoes.
2. Reduce the heat and simmer until the potatoes are tender. Test them with a fork.
3. Meanwhile, over low heat, place the cream and butter in a saucepan and heat until the butter melts, about 5 minutes.
4. Drain the potatoes and place in a large bowl.
5. Using a potato masher, mash the potatoes together with the butter and cream.
6. Add the sour cream and salt and pepper and blend into the potatoes.
7. Continue to mash potatoes to your preferred consistency.

Hints and Clues

It is a good idea to heat the cream and butter and then add it to the potatoes because adding cold ingredients lowers the temperature of the potatoes.

Keep your eye out for real red-skinned potatoes. If the red color rubs off on your fingers, try another store. Some stores dye the potatoes because they can charge more for the red ones!

Bacon-Tossed Brussels Sprouts

You Need

INGREDIENTS	AMOUNTS
Brussels sprouts	5 pints
Thick-cut bacon	12 slices, cut into small pieces
Onion	1 small, chopped
White wine vinegar	3 to 4 tablespoons
Butter	1 tablespoon
Salt and pepper to taste	

Get Cookin'

COOKING THE BRUSSELS SPROUTS

1. Peel any old or yellowed leaves off the brussels sprouts. Cut off the stems and rinse.
2. Steam or boil the sprouts in salted water until tender but still slightly crunchy, about 10 minutes.
3. Drain the brussels sprouts. Set aside.

COOKING THE BACON

4. Sauté the bacon over medium heat until it begins to crisp, about 5 minutes.
5. Remove some of the rendered fat.
6. Add the onion and sauté until it begins to wilt.
7. Add the pepper and sprouts to the bacon mixture. Toss well.
8. Add the vinegar and butter, stir, and season. Serve immediately.

I never actually knew that brussels sprouts grow on long stalks until I was preparing this book! Now I think they are so cool I grow them myself!

Orange Zest Cranberry Sauce

You Need

INGREDIENTS	AMOUNTS
Cranberries	2 12-ounce bags, fresh
Water	¾ to 1 cup
Orange juice	½ cup
Sugar	2 cups
Orange zest	1 tablespoon
Fresh lemon juice	1 tablespoon (½ lemon)

Get Cookin'

1. Place cranberries in a pot with the water and orange juice and bring to a boil.
2. Cook until the skins burst, about 15 minutes.
3. Add the sugar, orange zest, and lemon juice and return to a boil, then simmer the berries until the proper jellylike consistency is achieved, 25 to 30 minutes more (when it cooks it will thicken even more).

Hints and Clues

If it doesn't seem like there is enough liquid for the cranberries, you can add more water or orange juice as they cook.

Parker House Rolls
with American Spoon Pumpkin Butter

You Need

INGREDIENTS	AMOUNTS
Pillsbury dinner rolls	2 cans
American Spoon pumpkin butter	½ cup

Get Cookin'

1. Preheat oven to 400°F or as directed on the package of dinner rolls.
2. Unfold the dinner rolls and line them up on a cookie sheet.
3. Make a crisscross mark on the top of the rolls with a knife about ¼ inch deep into the dough.
4. Use a kitchen thermometer or other pointed device to make a hole in the side of the dough on each roll.
5. Cut the top off the corner of a plastic bag. (You have just created a pastry bag.)
6. Fill a small plastic bag with the pumpkin butter and place the tip inside the hole.
7. Squeeze about 1 tablespoon into the center of the rolls.
8. Cook as directed on package or until rolls start to brown.

Hints and Clues

You can use any flavored butter or spread to make your dinner rolls more your own—or even sprinkle them with fresh herbs.

American Spoon products are all natural foods made in my hometown, Petoskey, Michigan! They are the best ever!

Graham Cracker Crust Sweet Potato Pie

You Need

INGREDIENTS	AMOUNTS
Graham crackers	10, approximately 2½ cups
Granulated sugar	⅔ cup
Butter	10 tablespoons (1 stick plus 2 tablespoons), melted
Mashed, cooked sweet potatoes	3 cups, canned (9.3-ounce can)
Eggs	3 large, beaten lightly
Sour cream	½ cup
Fresh lemon juice	2 tablespoons
Ground ginger	1½ teaspoons
Cinnamon	1 tablespoon
Brown sugar	2½ tablespoons

Get Cookin'

1. Preheat oven to 350°F.
2. Combine broken-up crackers and granulated sugar in a food processor and process until smooth.
3. Add melted butter and combine.
4. Put dough into pie dish. First create the edges of the crust and then the bottom of the crust.
5. Bake crust for 10 to 15 minutes.
6. Let cool completely.
7. Turn oven down to 300°F.
8. Blend all remaining ingredients together in a food processor until smooth.
9. Pour filling into the cooled crust.
10. Put pie on middle rack of oven and bake for 1 hour or until top starts to crack and looks dry.
11. Let cool completely before serving.

Hints and Clues

Blend filling to a very smooth consistency.

Store sweet potatoes in dark cool places . . . they will last a lot longer that way!

Cheddar Cheese Crust Apple Pie

....

You Need

INGREDIENTS	AMOUNTS
Flour	3 cups
Sugar	¼ cup
Salt	¼ teaspoon
Vegetable shortening	⅓ cup, cold
Butter	1 stick (8 tablespoons), cut into small pieces
Cheddar cheese	1 cup (approximately 3 ounces), grated
Ice water	4 to 6 tablespoons
FILLING	
Tart apples	7, peeled and cored, ½-inch slices
Lemon juice	1 lemon
Brown sugar	2 tablespoons
Granulated sugar	2 tablespoons
Cinnamon	1 teaspoon
Cream	1 tablespoon
Cinnamon sugar	Enough to sprinkle over the pie

Get Cookin'

1. Preheat oven to 350°F.
2. Put flour, sugar, and salt in a food processor and pulse to combine.
3. Add shortening and butter and pulse until small clumps form.
4. Add the Cheddar cheese and pulse until dough resembles coarse meal.
5. Add 2 tablespoons of ice water at a time and pulse until the dough starts to clump and holds together when pinched.
6. Divide dough in half and wrap in 2 separate discs in plastic wrap. Refrigerate at least 1 hour.
7. Roll out 1 disk of dough into a 10½-inch circle on floured parchment.
8. Place crust in pie plate and refrigerate.
9. Roll out the remaining disk of dough, also on floured parchment, to a 10-inch circle.

Be sure your dough is well chilled before baking; chilled dough crisps better! Use cream, milk, or water to help seal the bottom crust to the top crust. Brushing the top crust with cream helps the crust to turn a nice golden brown.

10. Keeping it flat, refrigerate crust till ready to use.

11. Peel, core, and slice the apples and put in a large bowl.

12. Add the lemon juice, sugars, and cinnamon and toss.

13. Remove the refrigerated bottom crust and add filling, piling it toward the center.

14. Brush the edges with cream to help seal the top crust to the bottom and place the 10-inch crust on top.

15. Seal and trim the crusts, leaving 1 inch of overhang. Crimp as desired.

16. Using a sharp knife, cut vents in the top crust.

17. Brush the top and edges with cream and sprinkle with cinnamon sugar.

18. Bake for about 1 hour or until crust is golden and filling bubbles.

19. Serve when cool.

Hints and Clues

Rolling dough on floured parchment paper makes it easier to spread, and a piece of plastic wrap on top helps the dough not stick to the rolling pin.

13

Lunch in the Workshop

PROJECTS

Tool Table TABLE

Bolted NAPKIN RINGS

Buckets o' Goodies GLASSES AND PLATES

Flower Power CENTERPIECE

Bottoms Up PLACE MATS

Just Toolin' FAVORS

MENU

Oven-Fried Chicken
with a Garlic and Parmesan Crust

German Potato Salad

Chilled Asparagus Soup

Gingersnap Ice Cream Sandwiches

have you heard about feng shui?

Strictly speaking, it's the practice of living harmoniously with the energy of the surrounding environment, which naturally leads to the art of placement not only of buildings but of everything within them.

What does THAT mean?

Well . . . it's all the rage right now. I think it's always been big in the Far East but it's really catching on around here. People are having entire houses set up according to feng shui principles. Offices across the country are rearranging the furniture to create more efficient workplaces. They are hiring people to come in—not to decorate—but to decide which way a chair should face to be in accordance with nature. Hmm.

While I am sure that there is merit to feng shui, I've got my own way of feeling harmonious with nature and it's nothing that somebody else can tell me. For me, it's all about using your workspace in different ways.

It started at my gift store and café GOAT. After department store work, waitressing, and catering jobs, I found myself for the first time since school sitting in the same place every day. I loved my store so it wasn't a problem, but I was always happier after one of my friends dropped by. So I invented Friday night supper clubs, where I served a family-style supper to 30 people.

On Saturdays I always was happy because I had Friday nights in my mind to keep me company all day.

Now, when I am not shooting my show, I am in my workshop thinking up ideas and testing them. I've got to admit, though, sometimes the ideas just ain't flowing like they need to be. Skeptics of my own theory and feng shui fans would say it's because my shelves aren't properly oriented, or maybe my entire building faces the wrong direction. Well . . . I really like my workshop.

What do I do? I call my friends and say "Come on over. . . . " I put away my glue guns, my hammer, nuts, bolts, bulbs, pots, and paper and get to changing my worktable into a dining table. Sometimes I don't put my things away; I use them on my table. And guess what? Once again, the ideas start flowing!

Wherever you do your projects . . . your garage, your shed, your backyard, or your kitchen, bring your friends in. Let them see what you are doing and serve them some of the food you've been cooking! Not only will it be fun—it will bring a little more (or a lot more, depending on your friends) life into your space. You just may be surprised at what you come up with and no matter what, you'll have a good time.

Tool Table

You Need

SUPPLIES
Plywood
2 sawhorses
Peg-Board

TOOLS
Ruler
Large Sharpie

Get Started

1. Center plywood on top of the sawhorses.

2. Place Peg-Board on top of the plywood.

3. Set the place mats in their designated locations.

4. Draw an outline of the place mats, measuring 1½ inches away from all sides of the mat.

5. Do the same for your beverage tin up in the right-hand corner.

Hints and Clues

It's easier to draw the outline if it runs over the holes. That way, you are just connecting the dots!

Bolted

You Need

SUPPLIES

Large key ring that has a
    center hinge and fully opens
Bolts that slide over the
    key ring
Handi-Wipes

Get Started

1. Open the key rings.
2. Slide on the bolts, covering
the entire ring.
3. Snap the ring shut.
4. Slide in the Handi-Wipes.

Hints and Clues

We used Handi-Wipes to
further our theme, but any napkin will do! Try paper towels.

Buckets o' Goodies

You Need

SUPPLIES
Collection of tins
Denim fabric

TOOLS
Wax paper

Did you know that galvanized metal is rustproof?

Get Started

BEVERAGE TIN
1. Fill each tin halfway with ice.
2. Place a bottled beverage in each tin.

CHICKEN BUCKET
1. Line each tin with a piece of denim that has been cut into a square twice the size of the tin.
2. Cover the denim inside the tin with a piece of wax paper.
3. Put the chicken in the tin on top of the wax paper.
4. Wrap the chicken by tying together the opposite corners of the denim in a knot that meets at the center.

Hints and Clues
Collect old tins—round and square, short and long—at your local garage sales and flea markets.

Flower Power

Get Started

1. Fill the entire putty bin with dry oasis.

2. Cover the top of the oasis with the chain so that no oasis shows through.

3. Cut off several pieces of armature wire in varying lengths, anywhere from 2 feet to 5 feet long.

4. Bend the wire into the shape of flowers with stems.

5. Drive the wire stems in between the chain links and through the oasis for support.

6. Repeat in as many bins as you need to place down the center of the table.

7. Place bins down the center of the table.

Hints and Clues

If you do not have oasis, Styrofoam works well.

You can replace the chain link with nuts, bolts, screws, and nails.

> *It's a good idea to always keep your oasis in a plastic bag when you are not using it 'cause otherwise it gets all over the place!*

You Need

SUPPLIES

Metal putty mixing bins

Floral oasis

Chain

Armature wire

TOOLS

Wire cutters

Bottoms Up

You Need

SUPPLIES

Denim

Plywood cut into place mats

Large snaps

Blue jean pockets

TOOLS

Staple gun and staples

Hammer

Did you know that Levi's were worn first by coal miners in the West? They were the most durable fabric ever! Check out the label . . . there's a bit of history on every pair.

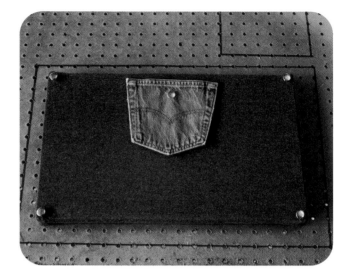

Get Started

1. Cut denim into pieces that will cover the top of the plywood placemats, leaving 3-inch borders on all sides.

2. Fold the extra fabric around to the back of the place mat, mitering the corners, and attach the fabric to the underside of your place mat using the staple gun. Make sure you pull the fabric tight as you go.

3. Attach a snap to all four corners by following the directions on your snap packages. (Make sure you buy snaps where the base screws in so that you can screw the base into the wood.)

4. Attach the bottom of a snap to the center of your place mat.

5. Attach the top of the snap through both layers of your pocket and connect with the bottom snap in the center of your place mat.

Hints and Clues

The pocket is a great place in which to slide silverware.

Make sure when you cut out your blue jean pockets that you leave them in one piece. The front and the back of the pocket both need to be cut out so that it can hold things.

Just Toolin'

You Need

SUPPLIES

Canvas tool belts

Collection of workshop
    supplies

TOOLS

Stamp with a blank space
    for a name
    (e.g., Received By,
    Property Of)

Ink Pad

Sharpie

> *I love sample-size prod-
> ucts! You can always
> afford them, and they
> are fun to use as testers
> and for travel. Also . . .
> when you're having
> some friends over, send
> them away with a few
> little things . . . it's fun
> to play with them!*

Get Started

1. Stamp each belt in a central location.
2. Write the name of each guest in the blank space (e.g., Received By [guest name]).
3. Stuff belts with workshop supplies and hang on the back of each guest's chair.

Hints and Clues

Try to collect your tool belt supplies throughout the year when things go on sale.
It is also nice to fill the tool belt with sample-size products; that way you can introduce
your guests to a lot of your favorite things!

Oven-Fried Chicken
with a Garlic and Parmesan Crust

You Need

INGREDIENTS	AMOUNTS
Garlic and Parmesan croutons	8 cups cubed, 2 packages
Dried thyme	4 tablespoons
Fresh parsley	6 tablespoons, roughly chopped
Eggs	10, lightly beaten
Spicy brown mustard	5 tablespoons
Olive oil	3 tablespoons
Flour	4 cups
Chickens	4, quartered
Salt and pepper to taste	

Get Cookin'

1. Preheat the oven to 425°F.

2. Prepare the "assembly line" of ingredients that you will use to coat the chicken for oven frying. First, place the croutons and dried thyme in a food processor and pulse until chopped roughly but not too small. For more control, chop with a knife. You want to keep some larger pieces intact for a more interesting and crunchy texture.

3. Transfer the crouton-thyme mixture to a large plate and mix with the parsley. Set aside.

4. Next, make the "glue" that will hold the crumbs on the chicken parts. In a bowl, whisk together the eggs, mustard, and oil.

5. To finish the setup, place the flour on a plate and set the three elements of the recipe (the flour, the egg mixture, and the crouton mixture) in a line.

6. Rinse the chicken parts under cool water and pat dry with paper towels.

7. Generously season the chicken skin and meat with salt and pepper.

8. Dredge a piece of chicken on both sides in the flour and shake to remove the excess.

9. Dip the flour-coated chicken in the egg mixture.

10. Then dredge the chicken on both sides in the bread crumb mixture, patting on more by hand if needed.

11. Place the coated chicken, skin side up, on a baking sheet.

12. Bake for 40 minutes, or until juices run clear when pierced with a knife.

What's the difference? Dredging means a thin or light covering with dry ingredients. Coating can be thick or thin liquid or nonliquid ingredients.

German Potato Salad

You Need

INGREDIENTS	AMOUNTS
Medium-sized red potatoes	10 whole, skins on
Bacon	8 slices
Onions	1 cup, diced
Celery	1½ cups, diced
Fresh dill	4 tablespoons, chopped
Fresh Italian parsley	3 tablespoons, chopped
Red wine vinegar	½ cup
Spicy brown mustard	2 tablespoons
Ground mustard powder	¼ teaspoon
Sugar	2 teaspoons
Canola or olive oil	½ cup
Salt and pepper to taste	

Get Cookin'

1. Place red potatoes in large pot and cover with cold water.
2. Bring the water to a boil and cook the potatoes until tender. When the potatoes are cooked, drain and let cool slightly.
3. Cook the bacon over medium heat until crisp, about 8 minutes.
4. Drain on a paper towel when crisp but reserve half of the bacon grease.
5. Using the same sauté pan with the reserved bacon grease, add the onions and celery and sweat until translucent, about 10 minutes over low to medium heat.
6. Slice potatoes in rounds about ¼ inch thick.
7. Break the cooked bacon in pieces and add to a bowl with the potatoes, onions, celery, dill, and parsley.
8. Add vinaigrette and toss to coat the potatoes.

VINAIGRETTE

9. Place the wine vinegar, brown mustard, mustard powder, and sugar in a blender.
10. Puree until incorporated, then slowly add the oil with the motor running until all has been added.
11. Toss with the potato salad and serve. Season to taste with salt and pepper.

Chilled Asparagus Soup

You Need

INGREDIENTS	AMOUNTS
Low-sodium chicken stock	6 cups
Asparagus	3 pounds (cut into 1-inch pieces and save the tops for garnish)
Unsalted butter	1 stick (8 tablespoons)
Leek	1, chopped
Garlic	3 cloves, finely chopped
Carrot	1 medium, cut into 1-inch pieces
Medium-size red potatoes	2, peeled, cut into 1-inch pieces
Salt and pepper to taste	
Cayenne	a pinch
Heavy cream	½ cup

Get Cookin'

1. Bring the stock to a boil in a medium-size saucepan.

2. Add the asparagus and cook for 10 minutes, or until tender.

3. While the asparagus is simmering, melt butter in a heavy-bottomed medium-size sauté pan.

4. Add leek and garlic, cover the pan, and sweat for 3 to 5 minutes.

5. Add the carrot and potatoes and cook 1 to 2 minutes.

6. Add cayenne and salt and pepper.

7. Add the vegetable mix to the asparagus and stock mix and simmer for 15 minutes.

8. Remove from heat and let cool.

9. Process in batches in blender until smooth.

10. When ready to serve, stir in heavy cream.

Sweating is a good cooking method to use when making soup. Because, when you sweat vegetables they do not brown and retain their color.

Hints and Clues

This soup can be served hot or chilled.

Garnish with asparagus tips, if desired.

Gingersnap
Ice Cream Sandwiches

You Need

INGREDIENTS	AMOUNTS
Gingersnap cookies	12 large, soft
Vanilla ice cream	1 pint
Chocolate chips	1 cup

Get Cookin'

1. Place gingersnaps on a parchment-lined cookie sheet.
2. Place ice cream in the bowl of a stand mixer and, using the paddle attachment, gently blend till ice cream is spreadable.
3. Using an offset spatula or a tablespoon, cover the bottom of 6 of the gingersnaps with ¼ cup ice cream, then place a gingersnap on top and gently press down.
4. Place the ice cream sandwiches in the freezer and let chill.
5. After 30 minutes, remove ice cream sandwiches from the freezer and gently roll the outside edge of the sandwich in a bowl of chocolate chips. Return the sandwiches to the freezer to harden for 30 minutes or until ready to serve.
6. When ready to serve, remove the ice cream sandwiches from the freezer and let them stand at room temperature for 5 minutes or so to soften up—but don't let them become too soft.

Hints and Clues

If you don't have a standing mixer, you can easily put the ice cream in a bowl and use a wooden spoon to mix it until it becomes spreadable.

14

Book Club Dinner

PROJECTS

Maptop TABLE

Corset NAPKIN RINGS

Serious Shades LIGHTING

Clearly Creative Coasters COASTERS

You Can't Tell a Book by Its Cover RUNNER

Shakespeare's Frost CENTERPIECE

Throne's Throw CHAIRS

MENU

Shepherd's Pie

Garlic Mashed Potatoes

Herb-Braised Carrots

Grand Hotel Pecan Balls with Fudge Sauce

Book Club Dinner

When i was in high school i elected to take

"Advanced Dramatic Works Class." I was pretty excited. It met for two hours a day, four days a week: what fun! Anything with the word "advanced" would surely help with those college applications.

I arrived in class ready to go. Sitting down in my chair, I looked up to find a sixty-something woman with black-rimmed spectacles hanging from a chain, standing in the front of the room. Who WAS this woman? All my other drama teachers were Cool with a capital C.

"My name is Gerta Taran; you may address me as Professor Taran. I have been teaching this class for twenty-nine years, and I need no help in doing it, so I don't welcome any suggestions."

She then directed us to the back of the room where there were piles and piles of books. *Who was this woman and what was this class?* "There are the plays we will read. Each student will

be expected to pick a major playwright and prepare a class long presentation on both the playwright and an original interpretation of one of his works. Get your books, we have work to do."

This was not what I had intended at all. I wanted to ACT, not read. Ugh. I don't remember any more of the first class, except for running to the pay phone after it was over and telling my mother I needed to transfer out of a class. PLEASE HELP! Dinner that night was less than successful . . . I begged both of my parents to get me out of this class. Pleeeeeeeeeease. NO way. UGH.

After the first month. it was time to start the in-class presentations. I had chosen Shakespeare as my playwright and *Hamlet* as my play. It was late November and I was skiing every day after school, so inevitably the report was not getting done. I figured I'd read *Hamlet* the night before and prepare something that morning in study hall. There was

plenty of information about Shakespeare in the back of the book anyway.

Well . . . let's just say that it wasn't that easy getting through *Hamlet*. What was easy getting through was research about the period itself . . . I loved learning about the banquets, the lighting, and the food. I was getting a bit panicked about the play, though, so I decided to wow Professor T. with a totally amazing presentation. I would sit the class down to Shakespeare's banquet and my report would go from there. I arrived in class an hour early with all my props, a huge amount of food that I had stayed up all night preparing, and very little knowledge of *Hamlet*.

Professor T. was less than happy having food in her classroom, let alone shepherd's pie, but my classmates had a ball. I'm not going to disclose my grade on the project, but I will say that it was well worth it!

Maptop

You Need

SUPPLIES
Maps

Plywood

Masking tape

Tea bags

Paper towels

Wood stain

1½-inch-wide wood trim

Finishing nails

TOOLS
Cotton rag

Handsaw

Hammer

Get Started

STAINING THE MAP
1. Spread the maps over the plywood so that they overlap the edges.

2. Tape the edges underneath.

3. Steep tea in boiling water until the water is very dark. Remove tea bags.

4. Once tea has cooled, wet the tip of a paper towel with tea and wipe the towel across the map to stain it.

5. Continue the process until desired contrast is obtained.

APPLYING THE TRIM
6. Stain the wood trim and allow it to dry thoroughly.

7. Cut the trim so that it will frame the tabletop.

8. Attach trim to the edge of the tabletop, hammering it through the map into the plywood.

9. Place the plywood on top of your table. (You may want to put some sort of pad in between your table and the tabletop so that the plywood does not harm your tabletop.)

Hints and Clues
For a deeper stain, wipe a wet tea bag directly onto the map.

Coffee could also be used in the map-staining process for a different look.

This is a great dinner for a book club. It's a good idea to put the group in the mood by making a meal that has to do with the book at hand. You can always start out with a maptop, pointed toward the location of the book the group is reading. After you read the book, let your imagination soar!

Corset

Get Started

1. Laminate the bookplate copies.

2. Cut the laminated bookplates into 5 x 3-inch rectangles.

3. Punch 4 holes down the long sides of the bookplates.

4. Lace the leather through the holes as you would a shoe.

5. Slide in a rolled napkin.

6. Tighten the laces and tie them off.

Hints and Clues

Pick bookplates that further the theme of the party.

You Need

SUPPLIES

Laminate paper

Color copies of a bookplate

Leather shoelaces

TOOLS

Scissors

Hole puncher

Before printing was streamlined, images in books were printed from hand-carved plates. They were set apart from the actual text by the kind of paper they were printed on. Now, they can be found at antiques fairs and are great framed in groups or alone.

Serious Shades

You Need

SUPPLIES
Galvanized tin funnels, 5½
inches in diameter
Candles
Candlesticks
Candle followers

TOOLS
Tin snips

*Keep your eye out for
candle followers at your
local craft stores.*

Get Started

1. Cut the spout off each funnel, using tin snips.

2. Bend the rough edges where you have just cut into the inside of the funnel.

3. Place the candle in the candlestick.

4. Place the follower over the top of the candle.

5. Put the funnel/shade on the follower.

6. Arrange the shaded candles down the center of the table.

Clearly Creative Coasters

Get Started

1. Adhere a sheet of clear laminate with masking tape to your work surface.

2. Press decorative stamp onto ink pad. Stamp image on clear laminate paper. Allow ink to dry.

3. Cut around the stamp, creating an appliqué.

4. Peel the laminate appliqué apart.

5. Center the appliqué on the precut glass coaster.

6. Apply the etching cream as directed.

7. Peel off the appliqué and rinse.

Hints and Clues

Taping the clear laminate to your work surface will prevent it from curling.

You Need

SUPPLIES

Laminate paper

Masking tape

Decorative stamps
  (we used a fleur-de-lis shape)

Ink pad

Coaster-size glass squares

Etching cream

TOOLS

Scissors

Rubber gloves

You Can't Tell a Book by Its Cover

Reading out loud can be a great after-dinner treat. Try marking particular passages in books and asking guests to read them after dinner.

You Need

SUPPLIES

Books of various sizes
White butcher paper

TOOLS

Scissors
Transparent tape

Get Started

1. Wrap each book with butcher paper as if you were making a book jacket.
2. Tape edges to secure.
3. Stack books in piles down the center of the table.

Hints and Clues

Brown paper and maps also make good book covers.

Make your piles in different heights.

Shakespeare's Frost

Get Started

1. Apply stencils letter by letter to each bottle until the name of choice is spelled on the bottles.

2. Apply etching cream as directed.

3. Peel stencils.

4. Fill each bottle ¾ way up with water.

5. Place a single flower in each bottle.

6. Line bottles up in the center of the table.

You Need

SUPPLIES

Adhesive stencils in Olde English font

Collection of vintage glass bottles

Etching cream

Long-stem fresh flowers (e.g., spider mums)

TOOLS

Rubber gloves

Throne's Throw

You Need

SUPPLIES

Specialty paper for printing
iron-on transfers
White pillowcases

TOOLS

Computer
Iron
Ironing board

Get Started

1. Open a word processing program on a computer.

2. Choose an appropriate font.

3. Create two- or three-letter monograms.

4. Select color of choice (if you have a color printer) and test print on a piece of paper.

5. Load specialty paper according to directions and print as many iron-on transfers as necessary.

6. Apply letters (according to iron-on directions) to the center of the top of pillow.

7. Slide pillowcase over the back of a chair.

Hints and Clues

Chairs with no arms work best for this project.

Lenox is the only U.S. full service premium tabletop company creating American china, crystal, linen, and silver. Maybe that's why they have created White House china for four presidents!

Shepherd's Pie

···

You Need

INGREDIENTS	AMOUNTS
Olive oil	3 tablespoons
Pearl onions, small and peeled	1½ cups, halved
Garlic	3 cloves, thinly sliced
Celery	¾ cup, chopped (approximately 2 stalks)
Mushrooms	2 cups, cleaned and sliced
Flour	3 tablespoons
Ground beef	2 pounds
Salt and pepper to taste	
Beef stock	1 cup
Tomato paste	3 tablespoons
Dried thyme	1½ teaspoons
Red pepper flakes	1 teaspoon
Flat-leaf parsley	½ cup (plus a bit for garnish), roughly chopped
Garlic mashed potatoes (recipe follows)	
Parmesan cheese	¼ cup, grated
Cheddar cheese	½ cup, grated

Get Cookin'

1. Preheat the oven to 425°F.

2. Heat olive oil in a large skillet over medium to medium-high heat.

3. Add pearl onions, toss, cover, and steam until they begin to soften, 5 to 7 minutes.

4. Add the garlic and celery and stir.

5. Add mushrooms and cook until they give off liquid and start to brown, approximately 5 minutes.

6. Add 1 tablespoon of flour, stir, and cook 1 to 2 minutes. Add meat, break it up, season with salt and pepper, and cook until browned.

7. Add stock, tomato paste, thyme, and pepper flakes and bring to a boil. Lower heat and simmer until gravy thickens and is absorbed by meat.

8. Stir in ½ cup parsley and remaining flour.

9. Pour filling in a deep pie dish and let cool.

10. Spread the mashed potatoes on top of the meat.

11. Sprinkle potatoes with Parmesan and Cheddar cheeses.

12. Bake pie for about 15 to 20 minutes.

13. Remove from oven and sprinkle with remaining chopped parsley. Let stand 5 minutes before serving.

Hints and Clues

Allow all the liquid to be absorbed by the meat and vegetables so it doesn't spill out later.

If you cannot find pearl onions, just chop and add the onions you have at hand.

You can use leftover cooked hamburger meat rather than raw, or make the meat a day ahead and reheat it before cooking.

Top the pie with the Parmesan and Cheddar cheeses to help with the browning process. As the cheese bakes, it makes a nice crust on top of the potatoes.

Garlic Mashed Potatoes

You Need

INGREDIENTS	AMOUNTS
Russet potatoes	4 medium to large, peeled and sliced
Garlic	5 whole cloves, peeled and smashed
Milk	1 cup
Butter	6 tablespoons
Salt and pepper to taste	

Get Cookin'

1. Place potatoes and garlic in a large pot and cover with cold water.

2. Bring to a boil and cook until tender, about 12 minutes. Check the potatoes by piercing one through the center with a knife or skewer to see if it is tender.

3. Drain.

4. While the potatoes are cooking, place the milk and butter in saucepan over low heat until butter melts.

5. Mash the potatoes and garlic in a Kitchen Aid mixer with the whip attachment.

6. Add the milk and butter and continue mashing.

7. Add salt and pepper to taste.

8. The potatoes will be used to cover the Shepherd's Pie (or they can be used alone).

Hints and Clues

Be careful not to overwhip because the potatoes will become sticky and gluey.

I like lots of salt and pepper in this recipe.

Herb-Braised Carrots

You Need

INGREDIENTS	AMOUNTS
Carrots	10, peeled and cut into 2-inch pieces on a diagonal
Low-sodium chicken stock	1 cup
Rosemary	2 stalks
Sage	6 leaves, roughly chopped
Butter	2 tablespoons
Granulated sugar	1 teaspoon
Salt and pepper to taste	

Get Cookin'

1. Place all ingredients except salt and pepper in a saucepan over low heat.
2. Cover and cook until tender, about 25 minutes. Check for doneness by piercing with a knife or skewer.
3. Season with salt and pepper to taste.

Hints and Clues

Discard the rosemary stem before serving.

Sugar brings out the natural sweetness in carrots. Bought a tough piece of meat recently? Try braising it . . . the slow-cooking process will seal in the flavor and also act as a natural tenderizer!

Grand Hotel Pecan Balls with Fudge Sauce

You Need

INGREDIENTS	AMOUNTS
Vanilla ice cream	1 Quart
Roasted pecan halves	2 cups
Heavy cream	1 pint
Sugar	½ cup
Light corn syrup	2 cups (16-ounce bottle)
Chocolate chips	1 pound
Vanilla extract	1 tablespoon
Crème de cacao	1 tablespoon

Get Cookin'

BALLS

1. Line baking sheet with parchment paper.
2. Scoop ice cream into a ball about the size of a baseball, perfecting the shape by rolling between your hands.
3. Roll each ball in the roasted pecan halves until well coated on all sides and place balls on the baking sheet.
4. When all balls are created, place in the freezer.

SAUCE

1. Combine the cream, sugar, and corn syrup in a sauté pan.
2. Bring to a boil.
3. Remove from heat and stir in the chocolate chips, vanilla extract, and crème de cacao. Let cool.
4. To serve, cover the bottom of a plate with approximately ¼ cup of sauce and place the pecan ball in the center of the sauce.

Hints and Clues

Make sure the ice cream is very cold before you begin.

At times you will have to push the pecans into the ball to make them stick.

If you cannot get roasted pecans, place pecans on a baking sheet in a 350°F oven for 6 to 10 minutes.

One of my favorite places in the world . . . the Grand Hotel on Mackinac Island. More than 50,000 Grand Hotel Pecan Balls are served each season.

15

It's All About You

A BIRTHDAY DINNER FOR SIX

MENU

Chicken Stew Pie with a Crusty Cover

Old-fashioned Succotash

Watercress and Apple Salad
   with Honey-Poppy Seed Vinaigrette

Chocolate Cake with Mocha Frosting
   and M&M's "Bing"kles

PROJECTS

Table with a View TABLE AND PLACE MATS

The Hot Seat CHAIRS

Chrysanthemum Cake CENTERPIECE

Face It GLASSES

Mouse Pads FAVORS

my brother Bing was born a day after me . . .

only eight years later. I'll never forget it. For an eight-year-old a birthday is a pretty big deal, especially when it is their own. Any interruption is—well—unthinkable! When you have two sisters, a brother on the way, and about a zillion relatives your birthday is the only single day of the year that everyone focuses on *you.*

The year Bing was born, my mother promised me—*promised* me—that nothing would ever get in the way of my day. I was sick of hearing about the new baby—a new room, presents, blah blah blah . . . I was tired of the new baby, and he hadn't even arrived!

My parents decided it would be too much to have a big birthday party that year, but we would have a special family dinner with me at the head of the table. Me me me me. . . . I couldn't wait.

When the day finally arrived, I thought school would never end. I mean *never!* My class

sang "Happy Birthday" to me, but there was no cake or presents. No fun at all. Finally . . . the last bell . . . the bus and HOME!

When the school bus pulled up in front of my house, I ran out across the front lawn, flew through the front door into the house. Wait a minute . . . where *was* everybody? *"Hello?"* What was that noise? The TV? I followed the sound and found Sandra, our sometime babysitter, in the den watching soap operas.

"Where's Mom?"

"Oh, your dad. He had to take your mother to the hospital."

The new baby???? This was *my* day . . . what happened to *me me me?* What was going on???

My sisters arrived home in time for dinner. My mother had thought to make parfaits and put them in the freezer in case the inevitable occurred. Great . . . for MY birthday we sat around the TV with our parfaits (mine did have a candle)

and watched *The Brady Bunch.* WHERE were my presents? I thought I was getting a new bicycle! Where was it?

The next day my dad called to say that I had a new brother, Bing, and all would be home soon. *Whatever,* I thought. Who cares?

Well . . . when they all got home—as you can imagine— MY birthday was not the big topic. I do have an image of my father giving me a new bicycle, but its bright red finish seemed dull; it just wasn't as rosy as those darn cheeks on my new brother.

For more than a few years it was Bing this . . . Bing that . . . Some say it took about twenty-one years for me to come to terms with it, so . . .

For Bing's twenty-first birthday I gave him a party. It was all about Bing—it was true—I was finally over it and to prove it, I pasted his picture all over the place. Everywhere!

Table with a View

You Need

SUPPLIES
14 x 11-inch photocopies of the
guest of honor
White butcher paper
Black plastic tubing
Upholstery tacks
Clear plastic vinyl
1-inch brass fasteners

TOOLS
Staple gun
Masking tape
Scissors
Ruler
Awl

Get Started

1. Photocopy a variety of pictures of your guest of honor. Make the photocopies at least large enough to fit under your plates (14 x 11) or larger.

2. Cover the tabletop with the white butcher paper and staple the overlap to the underside, using the staple gun. Depending on the width of your tabletop, you might need to use a couple of pieces. Flatten that seam with a long, clean strip of masking tape.

3. Attach the tubing around the perimeter of your tabletop with upholstery tacks. Nails or thumbtacks can also be used.

4. Cut a piece of the vinyl so that it covers the entire tabletop with an even drape around the perimeter of your table.

5. Cut additional pieces of vinyl into 16 x 13-inch rectangles to be used as place mats. *Note:* The vinyl should always be larger than the photocopied pictures.

6. Place the vinyl rectangles down on the table at each seat.

7. Using the awl, punch holes through each of the four corners of the place mats and then through the vinyl tablecloth underneath.

8. Push a brass fastener through the holes to attach the place mats to the tablecloth.

9. Slide the photocopies of the guest of honor between the place mat and the tablecloth.

Hints and Clues

If you can't find clear plastic vinyl at your local building supply store, buy a clear plastic shower curtain.

In place of photos you can always use comics, magazines, or newspapers.

The Hot Seat

Get Started

1. Lay out the letters of the name of the person who is to sit in the chair.
2. Glue the letters to the chair back.
3. Lay out the year of the person's birth.
4. Glue the date to the chair back.

Hints and Clues

If you don't have a lot of letters, think about using initials!

Collect mix-and-match chairs and give the guest of honor his or her chair as a gift . . . the more mixed and matched the chairs are, the more they can also stand alone!

You Need

SUPPLIES

Wood numbers and letters

Chairs

TOOLS

Hot glue gun

When we were very little, we each had our own chair. My sister Lynn, however, had her own rocking chair! Mine did not rock . . . I guess that's why I have a thing for rockers now!

Chrysanthemum Cake

You Need

SUPPLIES

Floral oasis

Rectangular-shaped floral trays approximately 1½ feet by 5 inches

15 bunches button mums

TOOLS

Floral knife

Floral snips

Get Started

1. Submerge oasis in a bucket of water until it is thoroughly soaked.

2. Place the oasis onto your floral trays.

3. Cut flowers, leaving a stem approximately 1 inch long—vary the stem lengths ever so slightly.

4. Push stems into oasis, covering the oasis entirely, top to bottom and front to back.

Hints and Clues

Varying stem lengths will create a great uneven texture that will add to the overall richness of your mum cake.

Feel free to use carnations or any other button flowers with a strong stem.

Face It

....

Get Started

1. Cut out the face you wish to use.

2. Take the picture to a copy store and have them copy it onto laminate paper or copy it yourself on a laser printer.

3. Cut the laminate into a circle around the oval of the face, leaving about a ½-inch clear border.

4. Adhere the images to the center of each glass.

Hints and Clues

Avoid the dishwasher!

Feel free to use any glass. With the help of a good remover substance, you can return your glasses to their previous condition anytime!

You Need

SUPPLIES

Pictures of the guest of honor's face

Laminate paper

Glasses

TOOLS

Scissors

Mouse Pads

You Need

SUPPLIES

Various images of the
guest of honor
Plain black foam rubber
mouse pads

TOOLS

Scissors

*Did you know that
without a mouse
pad, your mouse
will not be as
responsive.*

Get Started

Select the part of the images you wish to have imprinted on the mouse pads. Cut them out and bring them to the local copy store, where you can have them copied onto the top of the mouse pads.

Hints and Clues

Use them as coasters on the table.

Guests should take them home!

We had the images reproduced in black and white, but you can also have them reproduced in color.

Collect images that span the guest of honor's life so the mouse pads work as a timetable.

Chicken Stew Pie
with a Crusty Cover

You Need

INGREDIENTS	AMOUNTS
Chicken	5 cups, boneless and skinless, cut into bite-size chunks
Olive oil	6 tablespoons (4 for chicken, 2 for sweating veggies)
Cumin	2 teaspoons
Curry	2 teaspoons
Chili powder	1 teaspoon
Salt	2 teaspoons
Pepper	½ teaspoon
Celery	3 cups, cut into bite-size chunks
Carrots	3 cups, diced into ½-inch pieces
Red onions	2 cups, chopped
Potatoes	2 cups, cut into bite-size chunks
Peas	1 cup frozen, thawed
Low-sodium chicken broth	3 cups
Butter	6 tablespoons
Flour	6 tablespoons
Puff pastry	6 sheets
Egg	1, beaten

Get Cookin'

1. Preheat oven to 350°F.

2. In a skillet over medium heat, sauté the chicken in 4 tablespoons olive oil until cooked through, about 5 minutes.

3. Add the cumin, curry, chili powder, salt and pepper to the chicken and stir to coat.

4. Place the chicken in a bowl.

5. Over medium heat, sweat all the vegetables except the peas in 2 tablespoons of olive oil. (If your pot starts to burn, add a touch of water.)

6. Cook over low/medium heat in a covered pot for about 10 minutes.

7. Add the vegetables and the thawed peas to the chicken and mix.

MAKING THE GRAVY

8. Heat the chicken broth until it comes to a simmer.

9. In a separate pan, make the roux by heating the butter until it is foaming.

10. Add the flour and stir with a wooden spoon.

11. Continue to stir and cook the roux (flour and butter) mixture for about 5 minutes until it turns a light golden color.

12. Add the roux to the chicken broth and whisk well.

13. Bring to a boil and reduce to a simmer for 25 minutes until thickened.

14. When the sauce is ready, pour onto the chicken and vegetables and mix to coat.

15. Using packaged puff pastry dough, follow the directions on the package for thawing and unfolding on a lightly floured surface.

16. Place an empty serving dish upside down on the rolled-out dough and cut out a square to go into the dish. (It should be about 1 inch wider than the bowl so there is room to fold up the sides of the dish.)

17. Spoon in the potpie filling and then cover with another square of pastry that covers the top of the pie.

18. Pinch around the edges to seal and then brush the pastry lightly with beaten egg mixed with 1 tablespoon water. Place the pies on a sheet tray and bake in the oven for 25 minutes until the top is golden.

19. Allow the pies to stand for 5 minutes before serving.

Hints and Clues

You may not need to use all the gravy if it is looking too saucy.

You can cook the potpie in an ovenproof soup bowl . . . it looks great!

Origins: Did you know that meat stews with bread or pastry pies originated over 500 years ago in England?

Old-fashioned Succotash

You Need

INGREDIENTS	AMOUNTS
Butter	3 tablespoons
Yellow onion	½–1, or ¾ cup, chopped
Frozen or canned corn	1½ cups
Frozen lima beans	1½ cups
Heavy cream	½ cup
Paprika	1 tablespoon
Salt and pepper to taste	
Parsley	2 tablespoons, finely chopped

Get Cookin'

1. Melt the butter in a medium saucepan. Add the onion and sauté until soft but not brown, approximately 7 to 10 minutes.

2. Add the corn, lima beans, heavy cream, and paprika; season with salt and pepper and cook, stirring often, until the mixture thickens slightly, about 10 minutes.

3. When ready to serve, garnish with freshly chopped parsley and serve warm.

Hints and Clues

Make sure any frozen corn and lima beans are completely defrosted before you start cooking. Substitute low-sodium chicken broth or low-fat milk for a lower-calorie version of this dish.

Did you know that succotash is a fresh summer staple in the South? It's great for canning . . . a bit of summer all year long! If you like lima beans, try making a sojourn to the Cape May Lima Bean Festival held every October in Cape May, New Jersey.

Watercress and Apple Salad with Honey-Poppy Seed Vinaigrette

You Need

INGREDIENTS	AMOUNTS
Watercress	2 bunches, cleaned and torn into pieces
Apples	4, peeled, cored, and cut into ¼-inch slices
Lemon juice	Juice of ½ lemon

VINAIGRETTE	makes ½ cup
Dijon mustard	¼ cup
Honey	1 tablespoon
Apple cider vinegar	¼ cup
Canola oil	⅔ cup
Salt and pepper, to taste	
Poppy seeds	1 teaspoon

Get Cookin'

1. Place cleaned, dried, and torn watercress in a large bowl and set aside.
2. In a medium bowl, toss the sliced apples with the lemon juice.
3. Add the apples and lemon juice to the watercress.

Vinaigrette

4. In a small bowl or small food processor, combine the mustard, honey, and vinegar and stir to combine.
5. Slowly drizzle in the oil and whisk until well combined.
6. Season with salt and pepper.
7. Add the poppy seeds.

Try using watercress as a garnish—it will give a peppery taste to anything and it looks great!

Hints and Clues

Don't make salad too far ahead or apples will discolor and watercress could wilt.

Serve the dressing on the side or toss the watercress at the last minute so that the greens do not get soggy with the dressing.

Did you know that
the best way to frost a cake
is starting with the sides?
Try it!

Chocolate Cake
with Mocha Frosting and M&M's "Bing"kles

···

You Need

INGREDIENTS	AMOUNTS
Dark chocolate fudge cake mix	2 boxes
Milk chocolate	2 cups, or 1 24-ounce bag, very finely chopped
Unsalted butter	6 tablespoons, at room temperature, cut into small pieces
Instant espresso powder	5 teaspoons
Heavy cream	1 cup, plus 2 tablespoons
Apricot jam	1 12-ounce jar
Store-bought sugar letters	
M&M's	1 cup, crushed

Get Cookin'

1. Bake 2 cakes, following the directions on the cake mix box.

2. When cakes are done, let them cool on a cooling rack for 20 minutes and then invert.

3. When completely cool, trim cakes so they are flat and equal in proportion.

4. Place the chocolate, butter, and espresso powder in a medium pan and set aside.

5. In a separate pan, bring the cream to a boil over high heat. Pour the cream over the chocolate mixture.

6. Let mixture stand 5 minutes and then stir with a rubber spatula till smooth.

7. Refrigerate the frosting until cold and firm, approximately 1 to 2 hours.

8. Heat the apricot jam over medium heat till it is spreadable.

9. Put one cake round on a plate and slowly spread the apricot jam over the entire top of the cake round, and let harden 5 minutes.

10. Place the other cake on top, with the bottom facing up.

11. Using an electric mixer with the whip attachment, beat the frosting until it lightens in color and is spreadable.

12. Using a frosting spatula, gently spread the frosting over the sides of the cake first, being sure not to bring up crumbs.

13. When the sides are frosted, spread frosting on top of cake to finish.

14. Then take store-bought letters and place the letters spelling out the guest of honor's name on top of cake. Sprinkle crushed M&M's over the top of the pattern. This should spell out the birthday person's name.

16

Into the Woods

A BROWN FAMILY CHRISTMAS

PROJECTS

Ribbon Rings and Pinecone Cheer NAPKIN RINGS

Halos of Pine HEADDRESS

Ring Around the Candle LIGHTING

Pine and Cranberry Candle Cradle LIGHTING

Chairs Dressed in Their Christmas Best CHAIRS

Flavored Favors FAVORS

Run with It! RUNNER

Log Logic MENU

Snowflakes That Never Melt PLACE MATS

MENU

Spinach Salad
with Warm Bacon Vinaigrette

Classic Roast Beef

Red Wine and Fresh Blackberry Sauce

Roasted Root Vegetables
with Horseradish and Rosemary

Cranberry-Orange Upside-down Cake

what is Christmas really about? i didn't really know

until I was sixteen. I had gone through my childhood with the usual wonderful Christmas mornings, Santa Claus and all.

But, by the time I was sixteen we were done with that stuff. I was faced with having to buy other people presents. Although I would receive as well, I was no longer a child and was expected to give in turn.

My mother had opened a savings account for me and assumed that I was dutifully depositing my paychecks. Well . . . really the money was deposited somewhere between my job, the bank, the fudge stores, and the record store. . . . Little did my parents know that my savings account balance was only a bit more than when my mother started it . . . a grand total of $11.12, all belonging to my mother, anyway!

It was the week before Christmas and the area underneath the tree was beginning to fill with presents. Conspicuously missing was anything from me. Finally, I couldn't take the guilt so I bought myself

some time by telling everyone that their special presents would not appear until Christmas Eve. Of course this added to everyone's anticipation, but it at least gave me some planning time!

Alone in my room, I knew I *had* to do something. After racking my brain and looking through my closets and shelves for items that I could pass off as presents, I came up with zilcho! My parents had bought me every last thing in there! . . . I could hardly regift to my own parents.

Left with little alternative, I was forced to think about the holiday itself. What did it mean? I knew the most important part of Christmas was about giving, not receiving—or so my mother had told me! Therein was the problem; I had nothing to give.

Looking out the window at the old tree, I thought what a great life the tree had. It just got to be outside all the time and rest its branches in the air. I loved looking at it, it gave me total pleasure. *Wait a minute* . . . nature

never stops giving. Slowly but surely I realized that nature would give me all I needed to create a Christmas for everybody!

That very night I began to plan. I used large pieces of graph paper (supposedly for a math project) to graph out all of nature's gifts. For my mom, the very tree that gave the inspiration would be her gift. I made a to-scale diagram of the brass chandelier that hung over the dining room table. I figured out how many pine boughs I would need to cover it. For my father, hmm . . . well my father's job after dinner was always to clean the candlesticks and get all the drippings off; an arduous job after a long family meal with candlelight. For him, I made the pine cone bobeches that would not only look good, but they'd collect the wax drippings, saving him work! The rest was easy . . . I had gobs of maple syrup I gathered on a class trip. Favors for everyone! Dried fruit as napkin holders and, well . . . it all flowed from there.

Ribbon Rings and Pinecone Cheer

You Need

SUPPLIES
1-inch ribbon
Elastic
Pinecones

TOOLS
Scissors
Hole punch
Needle
Glue gun

Keep your eye out for pinecones on the ground! The best pinecones to use for crafts are those that have already fallen off the trees, not those still on the trees. Fallen cones are drier and have usually grown to maturity. You can collect them in the late fall and they will last forever!

Get Started

1. Cut a strip of ribbon that is 20 inches long.

2. Fold it in half evenly, making it 10 inches long.

3. Punch holes along the middle of the ribbon approximately every 1 inch.

4. Thread the elastic through the eye of the needle and weave it in and out of the holes, tying each end off with a knot. Pull tightly and scrunch it together (making something like a hair scrunchie!).

5. Glue the two ends together using the hot glue gun. You will need to make two scrunchies for each napkin ring.

6. Place one scrunchie around the medium-sized pinecone about halfway to three quarters of the way down. Glue the pinecone to the outer edge of the first scrunchie where the ends meet.

7. Insert the napkin and fluff the ribbon up.

Hints and Clues

French wire ribbon is easier to work with; it fluffs and holds its shape best! It is easiest to glue pinecones that have a flat bottom; you may want to trim or cut off the bottom to make it even more flat.

We glued the pinecone scrunchie to the end of the second ribbon scrunchie where the two ribbon ends come together, because this way you cover up the rough seams.

Halos of Pine

Get Started

FIRST TIER

1. Cut 4 pieces of wire, each 3 feet long, and attach the pieces of wire equal distances apart around the circumference of the large wreath.
2. Gather all 4 wires at the top, twist them together, and hang the wreath from your ceiling.

SECOND TIER

3. Cut 4 pieces of wire 1 foot long and attach each of the 4 wires equal distances apart around the circumference of the smaller wreath.
4. Hang this wreath beneath the larger wreath.

FINISHING TOUCHES

5. Cut strands of pine garland to cover the exposed wire on both levels and attach to wire with smaller pieces of wire.
6. Attach large pinecones sporadically around both wreaths.

Hints and Clues

The length of the wires holding your headdress in place will vary depending upon how high your ceiling is.
To keep your pine fresh longer, mist it with water once a day.

You Need

SUPPLIES

Spool of wire
30-inch pine wreath
20-inch pine wreath
Pine garland
Large pinecones

TOOLS

Wire cutters

Ring Around the Candle

You Need

SUPPLIES
3-inch metal washers

Moss

Small pinecones

TOOLS
Glue gun

Scissors

Get Started

1. Cover the washers with moss, using the hot glue gun.

2. After glue has set, trim the moss around the washer and glue the small pinecones on top of the moss around the washer with the top of the pinecone angled out (the pinecones are almost laying on their sides).

3. Glue a second layer of pinecones in between the caps of the first layer of pinecones, creating almost an overlapping look.

4. Fill in any spaces left between the pinecones with moss.

5. Trim up any excess moss with scissors.

6. Place on top of the candlestick and insert the taper.

Hints and Clues

Touch up your moss with green spray paint before using, if necessary.

Check the size of your washer to make sure it does not fall down the candlestick. It should rest right on the top.

Pine and Cranberry Candle Cradle

Get Started

CREATING THE POT

1. Hot glue pieces of pine all the way around a terra-cotta pot, allowing the greens to extend about 1 to 2 inches beyond the rim of the pot.

2. Tie a piece of sheer burgundy ribbon around the pine in a knot.

CREATING A PINECONE CIRCLE

3. Create a string of pinecones by wrapping the end of a piece of wire around the base of the first cone, moving over a few inches to wrap the next cone until you have a string.

4. Bring the two ends together, forming a circle the same circumference as the top of the pot.

FILLING IT UP

5. Insert the pillar candle into the terra-cotta pot.

6. Place the pinecone ring over the candle and let it rest on the rim of the pot.

7. Fill the space between the candle and the pot with loose cranberries.

Hints and Clues

Use various-sized pillars and pots to add interest to your tabletop.

You Need

SUPPLIES

Pine boughs

4-inch terra-cotta pots

Sheer burgundy ribbon

Wire

Medium pinecones

3 x 9-inch pillar candles

Cranberries

TOOLS

Glue gun

Wire cutters

Scissors

Chairs Dressed in Their Christmas Best

You Need

SUPPLIES
Chairs
Battenburg lace runners
2-inch-wide white grosgrain
ribbon
Battenburg lace cocktail
napkins

TOOLS
Glue gun
Scissors

While today lace is a luxury item, it started out as quite the opposite. Before garments were hemmed at the edges, they used to fray. People would weave the frayed edges of their clothing together to stop the fray from running. At about the year 1300, Philip IV of France saw the Flanders women weaving their fringes and brought the skill to his court. The rest is history!

Get Started

COVERING THE CHAIR
1. Cover each chair with a table runner.
2. Thread the 2-inch-wide ribbon through both sides of the runner where they meet on the back of the seat.
3. Tie them together around the arm of the chair.
4. Repeat on other side.

CREATING THE POCKET
5. Using a hot glue gun, attach three sides of a napkin to the center of the back of the chair cover, making the pocket.

Hints and Clues
We used Battenburg lace because it has larger holes so that the thicker ribbon can fit through the holes.

You can fill the pocket with any kind of holiday favor you choose, e.g., a bundle of mistletoe or a place card.

Flavored Favors

You Need

SUPPLIES
Small pinecones
Corks
Maple syrup
Glass bottles
½-inch-wide ribbon

TOOLS
Glue gun
Funnel

Get Started

PREPARING THE BOTTLES

1. Hot glue a small pinecone to the top of a cork.

2. Funnel the syrup into the bottles.

3. Snugly fit the corks into the bottles.

ATTACHING THE BOTTLES TO THE CHAIR BACKS

4. Cut a small piece of ½-inch ribbon, tie it around the neck of the bottle, and tie it off with a knot or a bow.

5. If the bottles become heavy and lean forward, put a drop of hot glue on the back on the ribbon that is on the neck of the bottle and glue it in place to the back of the runner. (The bottle can be removed by untying the knot.)

Run with It!

You Need

SUPPLIES
Garland or Princess Pine

Rose hips

Wire

Small pinecones

TOOLS
Garden clippers

Wire cutters

Get Started

1. Cut the garland to create three separate garlands that hang about 12 inches from the ground when placed across the width of your table, in between each place setting. (Think of them as running parallel to each other.)

2. Insert 3-inch-long pieces of rose hips all the way down the top of each runner. You should be able to work them in between the pine.

3. Wire together small clusters of pinecones, leaving enough wire on either end to twist around the garland.

4. Attach pinecone clusters along the garland every 12 to 18 inches.

Hints and Clues

Use a thin garland so it does not fan out across the table.

In my mind, wreaths and garlands are basic to Christmas . . . you can't have the holiday without them! Pick 'em up, string 'em up, or put 'em up . . . just do it!

Log Logic

SUPPLIES

Log

Card stock

1-inch roofing nails

Sprig of pine

Pinecone

Wire

TOOLS

Pen

Scissors

Hammer

Get Started

1. Use a log or piece of firewood that can stand upright.

2. Write up your menu on a piece of card stock with a beautiful pen, leaving a 2- to 3-inch margin on both sides. Cut off your margins so that your paper becomes more linear.

3. Use 1-inch roofing nails to attach the menu to the upright log at the top and the bottom.

4. Take a sprig of pine and a pinecone and wire them together, leaving a tail of wire.

5. Attach the pine and pinecone to the menu by twisting the wire tail around the nail at the bottom of the menu.

Snowflakes That Never Melt

Get Started

MAKING THE BASE

1. Use one whole stick as the middle piece.

2. Cut three other sticks in half.

3. Place 2 pieces on either side of the middle piece, creating a plus sign (+).

4. Place the other four halves in between the 2 cross-shaped pieces, creating an asterisk. (*) pattern.

5. Hot glue the pieces together in the center. You may have to glue it together more than once to keep the design together.

ATTACHING THE PINE

6. Cut sprigs of pine that are 8 inches long.

7. Cut off any small twigs along the branch except for at the ends.

8. If there are not "arms" at the tip of the branches, cut two small pieces of pine and glue them onto the end of your branch about 1 inch from the tip to create the arms.

9. Continue this pattern until all 8 sticks are covered with pine.

CREATING THE CENTER OF THE FLAKE

10. Cut several small pieces of pine similar to the arms you cut.

11. Starting at the center and working in a circular pattern, glue the short pieces of pine all the way around, thus creating a center to the snowflake.

Hints and Clues

When selecting the type of green you'd like to use, remember that something with a flat surface works better when plates are placed on it. We find Scotch pine works best.

To make the pine snowflake chargers last, keep them outdoors at night. When you bring them inside, mist them with water. You will be able to use them for a longer time that way.

Don't worry how your chargers differ from their neighbors . . . no two snowflakes are ever alike!

You Need

SUPPLIES

12-inch green wooden floral sticks

Bundle of Scotch pine

TOOLS

Glue gun

Clippers

Did you know that more snow falls each year in the United States and Canada than at the North Pole? The largest recorded snowflake was found in Siberia in 1971. It measured 8 x 12 inches.

Spinach Salad with Warm Bacon Vinaigrette

You Need

INGREDIENTS	AMOUNTS
Fresh spinach	3 pounds
Garlic clove	1, finely chopped
Sherry vinegar	6 tablespoons
Olive oil	½ cup
Salt and pepper to taste	
Thick-cut bacon	12 slices
Red onion	1, cut into ¼-inch rounds

Get Cookin'

1. Trim any tough stems from the spinach, discard any old leaves, and wash, drain, and dry.

2. Tear spinach into bite-size pieces and place in serving bowl.

3. Make the vinaigrette by whisking together the garlic, vinegar, and olive oil.

4. Season with salt and pepper to taste.

5. Cut the bacon into small cubes and fry until crisp, then drain on paper towels.

6. Discard some of the fat, add the vinaigrette to the pan, and gently heat up.

When warmed, pour over the spinach leaves and toss in the bacon cubes and onion.

7. Serve immediately.

Hints and Clues

Be sure the spinach is well cleaned.

I think every meal should have something green served with it.

The best way to check meat is with an oven thermometer. However, if you don't have one, here are some tests. . . .Use your index finger and lightly press on the meat in the center. If it is soft and dents easily but springs back to shape, it is medium rare. If it is rigid and dense, it's well-done.

If the meat is too hot to touch, try sticking it with a fork or the tip of a sharp knife. The juice that comes out will indicate the meat's doneness, red meaning rare, all the way to clear, meaning well-done.

Classic Roast Beef

You Need

INGREDIENTS	AMOUNTS
Brown sugar	¼ cup
Huckleberry jam	½ cup
Maple syrup	¼ cup
Salt	1 tablespoon
Pepper	2 teaspoons
Top round of beef	8 pounds

Get Started

1. Heat the oven to 400°F.

2. To make glaze, mix the brown sugar, jam, and syrup in a bowl until the sugar is fully incorporated.

3. Generously salt and pepper the roast and then use a brush to glaze the roast on all sides. Do not pour the glaze on the roast once it is in the pan, because the copious amounts of sugar will result in a burnt flavor later when you deglaze the pan for the sauce.

4. Place the roast in the oven and roast until the internal temperature reaches 130°F for medium rare, basting with pan juices while it cooks. Roasting times will vary, but generally it takes about 12 minutes per pound of beef. So for an 8-pound roast, it should take approximately 1 hour and 30 to 45 minutes.

5. Once the roast is done, remove from the roasting pan and let it stand for about 15 minutes to give the natural juices time to reabsorb into the meat. It will also continue cooking during this time.

Hints and Clues

Use a reliable cooking thermometer to measure the internal temperature of the roast. If you are using an instant read, pull the meat all the way out of the oven and make sure to push the thermometer into the center of the meat at its thickest part.

Be sure to continually baste the roast with the pan juices while it is cooking.

During the roasting, if the glaze starts to burn on the bottom of the pan, add a little beef broth or water to the pan but make sure the broth does not touch the beef. Only add enough to ensure that the sugar on the bottom stops smoking.

Red Wine and Fresh Blackberry Sauce

You Need

INGREDIENTS	AMOUNTS
Red wine	1 cup
Onion	½, finely diced
Butter	3 tablespoons
Blackberries	½ cup
Flour	3 tablespoons
Low-sodium beef broth	1½ cups
Salt and pepper to taste	

Get Cookin'

1. Use the red wine to deglaze the roasting pan when the roast comes out of the oven.

2. Use a wooden spoon to scrape the flavorful brown bits off the bottom of the pan. It is important that the roasting pan be hot for deglazing, so if your pan has cooled, place it over a high flame on the top of the stove until it becomes hot again and then pour in the red wine.

3. In a separate saucepan over low to medium heat, cook the onion in the butter until soft, about 4 minutes.

4. Add the blackberries and cook for another 3 minutes.

5. Add the flour and stir until the butter and flour are incorporated, about 2 minutes.

6. Pour the red wine from the roasting pan and the beef broth into the saucepan with the blackberries and onion and let simmer for about 5 minutes or until sauce reaches desired thickness.

7. Season with salt and pepper and serve.

Hints and Clues

The butter and flour used in this recipe are stirred together over heat to make a *roux,* which will thicken the sauce once the liquids are added.

Deglazing: When food is roasted or browned in fat, a "glaze" forms in the roasting pan or skillet. It is a result of the natural liquids that are released during the cooking of a protein. Glaze has a great flavor as long as it isn't burned. When wine, broth, water, or other liquid is poured on the glaze that sticks to the pan, it becomes easier to remove or loosen.

Roasted Root Vegetables with Horseradish and Rosemary

You Need

INGREDIENTS	AMOUNTS
Turnips	2, peeled and sliced in ¼-inch-thick rounds
Parsnips	2, peeled and sliced in ¼-inch-thick rounds
Acorn squash	3, seeds removed and sliced in wedges (skins can remain on)
Olive oil	½ cup
Horseradish (prepared)	3 tablespoons
Rosemary sprigs	5, leaves removed and chopped
Salt and pepper to taste	
Beets	2 bunches, stems removed and beets cut into ½-inch-thick rounds

Get Cookin'

1. Preheat the oven to 450°F.
2. Toss all the vegetables except the beets in the olive oil, horseradish, rosemary, salt, and pepper.
3. Place on cookie sheets serving some oil for the beets.
4. Do not crowd the vegetables or they will steam instead of roast.
5. Then toss the beets in the same bowl, coating with the remaining oil, rosemary, horseradish, salt, and pepper. (Keep the beets separate because they will bleed their color onto the other vegetables if tossed together.)
6. Place the beets on the cookie sheets with the other vegetables and roast in the oven for about 15 minutes or until the vegetables are tender when pierced with a knife or skewer.
7. Remove from oven, salt and pepper to taste, and place vegetables on a platter.

I think beets are the most beautiful of all the root vegetables as well as the most underutilized. C'mon . . . beet it!

Hints and Clues

Make sure the vegetables are thoroughly coated with oil before roasting.

Cranberry-Orange Upside-down Cake

You Need

INGREDIENTS	AMOUNTS
TOPPING	
Unsalted butter	¼ cup
Light brown sugar	⅔ cup
Grated nutmeg	¾ teaspoon
Light corn syrup	1 tablespoon
Cranberries (frozen or fresh)	2¼ cups
CAKE	
White cake mix	1 box
Orange juice	⅔ cup
Orange zest	1½ tablespoons (about 1 large orange)
WHIPPED CREAM	
Heavy cream	1 cup
Powdered sugar	2 teaspoons
Grated nutmeg	¼ teaspoon
Orange juice	2 tablespoons
TOOLS	
9 x 2-inch-high cake pan	

Get Cookin'

PREPARE THE CAKE

1. Preheat oven to 350°F.

2. Butter and flour an 8-inch cake pan.

3. Melt the butter in a medium saucepan and stir in the sugar, nutmeg, and corn syrup and cook until the sugar dissolves.

4. Pour the mixture into the cake pan and coat the entire bottom.

5. Add the cranberries in an even layer and really make sure the whole bottom is coated in cranberries.

6. Follow the cake mix instructions and substitute ⅔ cup of orange juice for the water in the recipe.

7. Add the orange zest and mix according to the instructions.

8. Pour the batter on top of the cranberries (you might have some extra; discard if you don't want it to overflow) to within one-quarter inch of the top.

9. Bake for 40 to 45 minutes.

10. Remove the pan from the oven and let cool.

11. Run a knife around the edges and place your serving plate on top.

12. Carefully hold the plate against the cake pan and invert it so that the bottom is up.

13. Gently lift the cake pan off the top of the cake.

PREPARE THE WHIPPED CREAM

14. In a mixer, beat the cream, sugar, nutmeg, and orange juice.

15. Beat until it is firm and reserve in the refrigerator.

Serve the cake with a scoop of cream.

Hints and Clues

A 9 x 2-inch pan is best for this cake.

Defrost cranberries if frozen.

Be sure that the cranberries are all the way at the bottom of the pan; the bottom should be covered.

Invert cake after 5 minutes, so topping drips and comes out easily.

Butter and flour sides, but not the bottom, of the cake pan.

> *Did you know that cranberries are grown in cranberry bogs found in wet, sandy coastal areas? They are freshest at the markets October through December. When cranberries are ripe, they bounce when dropped, giving them their nickname, "bounceberries." They have a very tart flavor, so most recipes calling for cranberries also call for a lot of sugar!*

Picture Index

Project List

CENTERPIECES

Misty Marbles, 27
AIRBORNE

Cactus Roundup, 46
LONE STAR

Bloomin' Pinwheels, 65
HOPSCOTCH

Stick in the Moss, 86
MAY DAY

Bag It!, 103
SIMPLICITY AND
SALAD

Desert Blooms, 122
SANTA FE FANTASY

Sandbox, 146
KATIE'S GREAT CALM
BY THE SEA

Colored Ponds, 165
THE COLOR GUARD

High Stakes, 189
KITCHEN GARDEN

Pot Luck, 226
THANKSGIVING

Flower Power, 255
LUNCH IN THE
WORKSHOP

Shakespeare's
Frost, 273
BOOK CLUB DINNER

Chrysanthemum
Cake, 288
IT'S ALL ABOUT YOU

CHAIRS

Egg Seats, 31
AIRBORNE

Ticking-Tac-Toe, 45
LONE STAR

Flowing like
a Ribbon, 82
MAY DAY

A Darlin' Garland, 102
SIMPLICITY AND
SALAD

Stumped, 126
SANTA FE FANTASY

Sitting Seaside, 144
KATIE'S GREAT CALM
BY THE SEA

Sea Legs, 170
THE COLOR GUARD

Pushin' for a Cushion,
203
ROMANCE IN THE
MORNING

Fall's Shawl, 231
THANKSGIVING

Throne's Throw, 274
BOOK CLUB DINNER

The Hot Seat, 287
IT'S ALL ABOUT YOU

Chairs Dressed in Their
Christmas Best, 306
INTO THE WOODS

Recipe List

BREADS

Skillet Corn Bread
with Jalapeño
and Pecans, 53
LONE STAR

Buttermilk Biscuits with
Cheddar Cheese, 92
MAY DAY

Oven-roasted Tortilla
Chips, 135
SANTA FE FANTASY

Quick Herbed Flat
Bread, 156
KATIE'S GREAT CALM
BY THE SEA

Herb and Onion
Focaccia, 175
THE COLOR GUARD

Savory Scallion and
Cayenne Scones, 193
KITCHEN GARDEN

Parker House Rolls
with American Spoon
Pumpkin Butter, 241
THANKSGIVING

DESSERTS

Blueberry Cobbler
with a Cornmeal
Crust, 18
THE ROCKWELL LIFE

Coconut Cookies, 37
AIRBORNE

Red, White, and Blue
Almond Shortcakes, 54
LONE STAR

Brownie Sundaes with
Creamy Butterscotch
Sauce, 77
HOPSCOTCH

Almond Apricot
Tart, 95
MAY DAY

Rhubarb-Ginger
Pie, 117
SIMPLICITY AND
SALAD

Caramel Flan, 136
SANTA FE FANTASY

Strawberry Fool, 158
KATIE'S GREAT CALM
BY THE SEA

Tiramisù Piled High, 178
THE COLOR GUARD

Zesty Lemonies, 196
KITCHEN GARDEN

Spiced Poached
Pears, 215
ROMANCE IN THE
MORNING

Chocolate Truffles for
Two, 216
ROMANCE IN THE
MORNING

Graham Cracker Crust
Sweet Potato Pie, 244
Cheddar Cheese Crust
Apple Pie, 245
THANKSGIVING

Gingersnap Ice Cream
Sandwiches, 262
LUNCH IN THE
WORKSHOP

Grand Hotel Pecan
Balls with Fudge
Sauce, 280
BOOK CLUB DINNER

Chocolate Cake with
Mocha Frosting and
M&M's "Bing"kles, 297
IT'S ALL ABOUT YOU

Cranberry-Orange
Upside-down Cake, 320
INTO THE WOODS

GRAINS AND LEGUMES

Rice and Currants, 34
AIRBORNE

Tabbouleh
Katie's Way, 112
SIMPLICITY AND
SALAD

Black Bean Cakes, 132
SANTA FE FANTASY

MAIN DISHES

Grilled Vegetable
Sandwich with a Pesto
Mayo, 13
THE ROCKWELL LIFE

Scallops with Ginger-
Scallion Sauce, 32
AIRBORNE

Chili-Rubbed Flank
Steak, 49
LONE STAR

The Leaning Tower of
Cheese, 71
HOPSCOTCH

Ham with Garlic and
Rosemary, 90
MAY DAY

Snapper
en Papillote, 110
SIMPLICITY AND
SALAD

BBQ Pork Marinated
in Tequila and
Coriander, 130
SANTA FE FANTASY

Steamed Cod with
Mango and Avocado
Relish, 152
KATIE'S GREAT CALM
BY THE SEA

Carpaccio, Arugula, and
Parmesan Stacks, 172
THE COLOR GUARD

Olives, Tomatoes, and
Zucchini Red Sauce
over Fettuccine, 176
THE COLOR GUARD

Soft Scrambled Eggs
with Goat Cheese and
Chives, 190
KITCHEN GARDEN

Skewered Poached
Salmon, 195
KITCHEN GARDEN

Challah French Toast
with Vanilla and
Nutmeg, 212
ROMANCE IN THE
MORNING

Roast Turkey, 235
THANKSGIVING

Oven-Fried Chicken
with a Garlic and
Parmesan Crust, 258
LUNCH IN THE
WORKSHOP

Shepherd's Pie, 277
BOOK CLUB DINNER

Chicken Stew Pie with
a Crusty Cover, 291
IT'S ALL ABOUT YOU

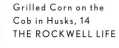

Classic Roast Beef, 315
INTO THE WOODS

VEGETABLES

Grilled Corn on the
Cob in Husks, 14
THE ROCKWELL LIFE

Fresh Tomato Salad, 17
THE ROCKWELL LIFE

Mustard Greens
Sautéed with Water
Chestnuts, 35
AIRBORNE

Lone Star Coleslaw, 50
LONE STAR

Spicy Onion Rings, 72
HOPSCOTCH

Three-Bean Salad with
Mustard-Tarragon
Dressing, 73
HOPSCOTCH

Fresh Peas with
Cream, 93
MAY DAY

Mrs. Brown's Scalloped
Potatoes, 94
MAY DAY

Fennel and Orange
Salad, 114
SIMPLICITY AND
SALAD

Spicy Carrot Salad, 115
SIMPLICITY AND
SALAD

Roasted Corn Salsa, 134
SANTA FE FANTASY

Gazpacho, 155
KATIE'S GREAT CALM
BY THE SEA

Sugar Snap Peas
Dressed with
Tarragon, 157
KATIE'S GREAT CALM
BY THE SEA

Sautéed Spring
Spinach, 194
KITCHEN GARDEN

Walnut, Sausage, and
Apple Stuffing, 236
THANKSGIVING

Smashed Red Skin
Potatoes, 238
THANKSGIVING

Bacon-Tossed
Brussels Sprouts, 239
THANKSGIVING

Orange Zest
Cranberry Sauce, 240
THANKSGIVING

German Potato Salad,
260
LUNCH IN THE
WORKSHOP

Chilled Asparagus
Soup, 261
LUNCH IN THE
WORKSHOP

Garlic Mashed
Potatoes, 278
BOOK CLUB DINNER

Herb-Braised
Carrots, 279
BOOK CLUB DINNER

Old-fashioned
Succotash, 294
IT'S ALL ABOUT YOU

Watercress
and Apple Salad with
Honey–Poppy Seed
Vinaigrette, 295
IT'S ALL ABOUT YOU

Spinach Salad with
Warm Bacon
Vinaigrette, 312
INTO THE WOODS

Roasted Root
Vegetables with
Horseradish and
Rosemary, 317
INTO THE WOODS